Sigrid Estrada

PAUL AUSTER is the bestselling author of *Travels in the Scriptorium, The Brooklyn Follies, Oracle Night,* and *The Book of Illusions,* among many other works. In 2006 he was awarded the Prince of Asturias Prize for Literature and inducted into the American Academy of Arts and Letters. His work has been translated into more than thirty languages. He lives in Brooklyn, New York.

# the inner life of
# Martin Frost

## Paul Auster

Picador

Henry Holt and Company

New York

www.picadorusa.com

Picador® is a U.S. registered trademark and is used by Henry Holt and Company
under license from Pan Books Limited.

For information on Picador Reading Group Guides,
please contact Picador.
Phone: 646-307-5259
Fax: 212-253-9627

E-mail: readinggroupguides@picadorusa.com

ISBN-13: 978-0-312-42703-0
ISBN-10: 0-312-42703-4

First Edition: June 2007

10  9  8  7  6  5  4  3  2  1

*The Making of*

# the inner life
# of martin frost

Céline Curiol:* You already wrote part of Martin Frost's story in *The Book of Illusions.* Why go back to it, expand it, and turn it into a screenplay?

Paul Auster: *The Inner Life of Martin Frost* has had a rather complicated history. In 1999, I was approached by a German producer to make a thirty-minute film for a series she was putting together of twelve short films by twelve different directors on the subject of men and women, so-called Erotic Tales. I was intrigued by the proposal and decided to take the plunge. It was early in the year, I remember, February or March, and I sat down and wrote my little script, which came to about thirty pages. Since the budget was going to be low, I confined myself to just two actors and one location—an isolated house in the country. The story of Martin Frost, a writer, and a mysterious woman who turns out to be his muse. A fantastical story, really, more or less in the spirit of Nathaniel Hawthorne. But Claire isn't a traditional muse. She's an embodiment of the story Martin is writing, and the more he writes, the weaker she becomes—until, when he comes to the last word of the text, she dies. He finally figures out what has been happening and burns the manuscript in order to bring her back to life. That's where the short version ended—with Martin bringing Claire back to life.

*Novelist, essayist, and journalist Céline Curiol is the author of two novels, *Voix sans issue* (translated into English as *Voice Over*) and *Permission,* as well as a nonfiction book about Sierra Leone, *Route Rouge.*

CC: What was the response from the German producer?

PA: Very positive. Everyone liked the script, and I went ahead and began making preparations to shoot the film. Willem Dafoe and Kate Valk—the great actress from the Wooster Group—were going to be my cast. Peter Newman, the producer of all the previous films I'd worked on, was again going to produce. We made an itemized budget and were starting to look for a house to film in when negotiations with the German company broke down. They wanted to release the money to us in three stages. One-third on signing the contract, one-third when we started shooting, and one-third when we were finished—and they approved the film. This last point worried me. What if they didn't like what I did and rejected the results? One-third of the budget would be lacking, and suddenly Peter would be in the position of having to pay off tens of thousands of dollars from his own pocket. I didn't want to put him at risk like that, so I backed out of the project. The thing that clinched it for me was a conversation I had with Hal Hartley. He had just finished shooting one of the twelve films for the series, and lo and behold, the German producer was insisting that he make changes, putting Hal in exactly the same mess I was afraid of getting us into. His advice to me was to pull out, and that's what I did. In the end, it was probably all for the best. For the fact was that not long after I finished writing the short version of *Martin Frost,* I began thinking I should extend it into a full-length feature film. Martin brings Claire back to life—and then what? That's where the story would start to get even more interesting, I felt. So I sketched out a plan for the rest of the film—nothing definite yet, but a stack of notes to mull over for the future. Then I put it all away and started writing *The Book of Illusions,* which had been brewing inside me for a long time, close to ten years. That was the summer of 1999, and I finished the manuscript two years later, exactly one month before the attack on the World Trade Center. Toward the end of the book, David Zimmer, the narrator, gets to see one of Hector Mann's late films shot in the New Mexico desert. For numerous reasons, *The Inner Life of Martin Frost* seemed to be the perfect story to use at this point in the novel, so I adapted the short version of the script and put it in.

CC: Did you make many changes?

PA: Nothing essential, really. The action had to be shifted to 1946, for example. The location had to move to Hector's house in New Mexico. The film had to be shot in black and white, and I had to abandon the scenario form and describe the film in prose. Quite a challenge, I might add. Those changes aside, however, the film in the book is very close to the original screenplay.

CC: Why didn't you incorporate the longer version into the novel?

PA: I was tempted, but I decided it would take too many pages to do it right, and in the process I would throw off the balance of the narrative.

CC: Why did it take you three years to go back to *Martin Frost* after you finished the novel?

PA: There were other books I wanted to write, books I had been thinking about for many years, and I was reluctant to leave my room. . . . Now that I think about it, September eleventh probably had something to do with it as well. It hit me very hard, watching it happen from the window of my house in Brooklyn, and the idea of making another film lost its attraction for a while. I wanted to be alone, to think my own thoughts. Directing a film means giving up a good two years of your life, and except for the writing of the screenplay, you're working with other people all the time. I just wasn't in the mood for that.

CC: What changed your mind?

PA: *The Brooklyn Follies* was the fourth novel I'd written in six years, and I think I was feeling a little burned out, not ready to start writing another work of fiction. And *Martin Frost* was still on my mind. I hadn't been able to get rid of the story, so one fine day I decided to take a crack at finishing it.

CC: The entire movie takes place out in the countryside, in a very isolated house. What was the appeal of that isolation, and what importance does it have in the film?

PA: To be very blunt, it was largely a question of money. If I was going to get a chance to make another film, I knew it would have to be done on a small scale, with an extremely limited budget. That's why I wrote it for just four actors and used just three locations: the house and the grounds of the house; the empty road; and for three days at the end of production, a soundstage, where we filmed the dream sequences and the shots of the spinning typewriter. I was trying to be realistic. I'm proud of *Lulu on the Bridge,* but it turned out to be a commercial failure, and I understood how difficult it would be for me to raise money for a new project. So, to quote a line from Fortunato in the film, I forced myself to "think small." But when it comes to the isolation of the setting—to answer your question at last—I wanted to create an otherworldly ambiance, a place that could be anywhere, a place that felt as if it existed outside time. The action unfolds in Martin's head, after all, and by choosing the house I did, a little domain cut off from the rest of the world, I felt I would be enhancing the interiority of the story.

CC: Why did you shoot in Portugal?

PA: Because the producer of the film, Paulo Branco, is Portuguese. I met Paulo fourteen or fifteen years ago in Berlin—through Wim Wenders, a mutual friend—and we've stayed in touch ever since. After *Lulu on the Bridge,* he told me that if I ever wanted to make another film, all I had to do was call him, and he would produce it. When the script for *Martin Frost* was finished, I called. We explored the possibility of shooting here in America, but we simply couldn't find enough money to do it. Paulo has made close to two hundred movies all over Europe, but Portugal is his home base, and he has all the means at his disposal to work inexpensively there—access to equipment, labs, crew, the whole works—and so we decided to go there. You watch the finished film, and you don't really know where you are. To me, it looks like Northern California. And all the props in the movie are American: the brown grocery bag, the house keys, the yellow legal pad, the eight-and-a-half-by-eleven typing paper, the license plates, the books on the shelves, everything.

CC: You put together quite an ensemble of actors. How did you go about casting the film?

PA: In November 2004, just when I was about to start writing the screenplay, I went to France to give a reading tour in five or six cities. In each theater, I would read a couple of paragraphs in English, and then a French actor would read the same passage in translation—and back and forth we'd go until the reading was finished. When my French publisher asked me which French actor I'd like to work with, I suggested Irène Jacob. I had met Irène in 1998 when I went to the Cannes Film Festival with *Lulu on the Bridge.* One afternoon, we wound up sitting next to each other at lunch, and we had a very good talk. When you see her act in a film like *Red* or *The Double Life of Véronique,* her talent and presence on screen are remarkable, but I found her just as remarkable in life. There's a special quality to Irène, something I've never seen in anyone else. A kindness, a goodness, a tenderness—I don't know what to call it—along with a terrific sense of humor and a startling lack of egoism, which is almost unheard of in an actor. In short, she's an exceptional person, and I wanted her to read with me. She happened to be eight months pregnant with her second child at the time, which meant she couldn't go on the tour, but we did the reading in Paris together. A couple of nights later, she invited me to a play she was performing in (yes, acting while eight months pregnant!), and after the play we went out for a drink with some friends. It was raining that night, and she offered to drive me back to my hotel in her car. That was when lightning struck. I looked over at her as she sat behind the wheel, and I realized that I was looking at Claire, the one and only Claire. I said to her: "I'm about to start writing a screenplay, and I think I have a part for you. Would you be interested in reading it when I'm finished?" She said she would, and when I finished in February, I mailed her the script. A few days later, she called me in New York and said she was in.

CC: What about the others?

PA: Michael Imperioli had auditioned for *Smoke* in 1994, and even though we didn't hire him, I was very impressed by his work. I gave him a small part in *Lulu on the Bridge*, but then something bigger came along for him, and I had to let him go. But I always hoped that one day we would wind up working together. He's made a great success in *The Sopranos*, of course, but he told me that the movie scripts he's sent are uniformly dismal. Cops and robbers, always a cop or a robber, and he turns them all down. He's so much better than that, with so much more range and intelligence. When I sent him *Martin Frost*, he accepted right away. One reading, and he was in. As for Sophie, I didn't meet with any resistance either. I know that some people will say I cast her because she's my daughter, but that's not true. There's no one who could have played the part better than she does—an eighteen-year-old who can both act and sing at that level. I feel lucky to have gotten her at the beginning of what promises to be a fine career. You never know in this business, of course, but there's a good chance that it won't be long before people stop thinking of her as my daughter and refer to me as her father.

CC: And your leading man?

PA: Every movie has its problems, and casting Martin proved to be the biggest problem of all. My first choice was Willem Dafoe, who was going to play Martin for the short version in 1999, but he was unavailable. A couple of good actors then turned me down. After that, someone very good accepted with a lot of enthusiasm, but then we ran into scheduling difficulties, and he had to back out. Finally, I found someone else and thought we were home free. The film was set to begin shooting on May eighth. In February, I went to Portugal for the first time and found the house with my first assistant director, Zé Maria Vaz da Silva, and the production designer, Zé Branco. Then I returned to New York and worked for the next month with the costume designer, Adelle Lutz, on wardrobe choices for the four actors. The plan was for me to go back to Portugal on April first to begin preproduction. On March fifteenth, just two weeks before I was supposed to leave, Adelle and I did a wardrobe fitting with the actor who was going to play Martin. Something wasn't right. He was very agitated, not at all himself, and then Adelle and I learned that he was in a bad spot financially. We were making the movie for next to nothing, and all the actors had agreed to work for minimum salaries. Now, suddenly, my distraught Martin let it be known that he couldn't do the part for so little and needed more money. What could I do? I understood his dilemma, but there was no way we could satisfy his demands. Fortunately, we parted on amicable terms.

CC: How did David Thewlis enter the picture?

PA: That evening, I asked myself the question: if I could get any English-speaking actor in the world to play the part, who would I want? The answer was: David Thewlis. I had met David only once, all the way back in 1997, when I was a member of the jury at Cannes. Mike Leigh was also on the jury that year, and one morning as we were walking along somewhere, David happened to pass by, and Mike introduced us. After that, David and I talked for a little while, and I remember being very touched when he told me that the last three novels he had read had all been written by me. All well and good. At least David Thewlis knew who I was. But how to get in touch with him without going through an agent? And how could I hope that an actor of his ability would be available? I contacted Heidi Levitt in Los Angeles, the casting director who had worked on *Smoke, Blue in the Face,* and *Lulu on the Bridge,* and asked her if she knew someone who could give her David's number. Yes, she said, she thought there was someone, and half an hour later she called back with the number. A promising start. The next morning, I called David in London and left a message on his cell phone. He called back several hours later, and the first thing he told me was that when he heard my message he thought that one of his friends was playing a prank on him. It turned out that for the past several weeks David had been asking around for my telephone number in order to contact *me.* There was a complicated and funny story he wanted to tell me about one of my books, and he couldn't believe that I had contacted *him.*

CC: And then?

PA: The script was e-mailed to David, and the next day he accepted the part. It felt like a miracle, a stroke of astonishing luck. Two and a half weeks later, we met for the first time in Lisbon. He and Irène had both come to rehearse with me for several days, and we hit it off immediately. Not only is he a superb actor, he's an irresistible person: intelligent, funny, a great raconteur, and kind to everyone around him. And—here's where it really starts to get interesting—he's a writer. For five or six years prior to playing a novelist in my movie, David had been writing a novel of his own. Incredibly, he finished the manuscript while we were all in Portugal, just before the first day of shooting.

CC: What were some of the problems you ran into while making the film?

PA: I lost my American DP in early April, just one week before he was supposed to join me in Portugal. Paulo sprang right into action and saved the day by finding me Christophe Beaucarne. As soon as Christophe accepted the job, I flew to Paris to meet him. We talked for six or seven straight hours, going over the thirty-page shot list I had put together in New York with the other DP. This is not to denigrate the man who backed out, but at this point I can't imagine having made the film with anyone other than Christophe. He's smart, fast, sensitive, and experienced. And physically one of the strongest people I've ever known. He was born in Belgium, and after a while David started calling him "Muscles from Brussels." David also told me (and this is someone who's appeared in close to forty films) that Christophe was the best DP he ever worked with. So, another problem solved at the last minute. And then, more recently, after the film had been shot and I returned to New York to begin working with my editor, Tim Squyres, I lost the composer who had agreed to write the score. Music is an essential part of the film. There's more than forty minutes of it in *Martin Frost,* and just when he was supposed to start working, the composer bailed out on me because he was backed up on another project—which, rest assured, was paying him a lot more money than our poor little movie ever could. And so there I was, stuck again, trying to think of a replacement. Two or three days later, Sophie turned nineteen, and Wim Wenders called to wish her happy birthday. He's known her since she was a little tot, and they're very fond of each other. As it happened, I picked up the phone, and before I passed the receiver to Sophie, I told Wim about losing my composer and asked if he had any suggestions. He did. A man named Laurent

Petitgand, who had written the circus music for *Wings of Desire* and the scores for several of Wim's movies, including *Far Away, So Close!* Dear Wim. He was the one who introduced me to Paulo Branco, and now he had just given me my composer. I called Laurent right away, and when he said he was interested in the job (low pay or not), Tim and I express-mailed him a DVD of a rough cut of the film. Laurent watched it, and the next thing I knew, he was in. Like everyone else who wound up working on this project, he accepted immediately, was undeterred by the minuscule salary, and did an outstanding job. I think his score is exceptionally beautiful.

CC: You wore two hats on this movie: writer and director. What are the advantages of doing both? What are the disadvantages?

PA: To tell the truth, I can't think of a single disadvantage. I'm not a full-time filmmaker, after all, and I tend to think of my occasional forays into the world of movies as an extension of my work as a novelist, as a storyteller. Not all stories should be novels. Some should be plays. Some should be films. Some should be narrative poems. In the case of *Martin Frost,* it was conceived as a film from the start—just as *Smoke* and *Lulu on the Bridge* were. By directing my own screenplay, I profit from the fact that I know the text better than anyone else. I know the rhythm of the words, the rhythm of the images, and I can communicate these things directly to the actors and the crew.

CC: You worked with a British actor and an American actor, a French actress and an American actress. Your crew was Portuguese. Your DP was French. Let's call it an international team. Was communication difficult at times? Was it a help or a hindrance to be collaborating with people who had different working methods?

PA: Actually, communication was never a problem. Three languages were spoken on the set, but English was the principal language. Both

Irène and Christophe speak English well, and most of the Portuguese crew had fairly good English. The ones who didn't know English knew French, but since I speak French, there wasn't any difficulty. I made a point of speaking in English with Irène from the first moment she accepted the part—to keep her immersed in the language of the film—but naturally, when she and Christophe had a one-on-one conversation, they spoke French. The same with the crew. They spoke in Portuguese with one another, but either in English or in French with me and the actors. There were some funny moments, of course. Zé Maria, the first AD, calling out before each scene: "Let's rehearsal!" Or Diana Coelho, the line producer, trying to explain to me that she and another woman were the same age, uttering this immortal sentence: "She has my old." But I understood exactly what she meant. We were such a small group—the working crew was only about eighteen people—we all became quite close, and while everyone worked very hard—*very hard*—there was a lot of laughter and goodwill on the set. As for different working methods—all very interesting to me, but since film is an international medium, a universal language, really, the differences are rather nuanced. An alternate method for numbering setups in a scene, for example, or the slightly different way the script supervisor wrote up her continuity reports. But there were also many advantages. In America, union rules forbid a DP from operating the camera. Not so in Europe—so Christophe operated himself. And while there's no union in Portugal, there are nevertheless certain unwritten rules. Eleven-hour days, with one hour for lunch. In America, crews work twelve hours. But only five days a week, whereas in Portugal we worked six.

CC: What was your biggest surprise on the set?

PA: The passion and intensity of the crew. The crews I've worked with in America have all been good, but much larger, and so inevitably a lot of people wind up standing around and doing nothing for long stretches of time. Because we were so small, everyone was busy from the beginning of the day to the end. People didn't walk, they ran. I was impressed by how knowledgeable they were and how much they accomplished. In some cases, one person would do the work normally done by three or four people on an American set. I myself like to work intensely, to keep pushing things along. I'm very decisive (I know what I want!), and I'm a stickler for details. The crew seemed to enjoy working at that rhythm, and we actually managed to shoot the film in twenty-five days, not twenty-nine days as originally planned. That allowed me to give the crew two Saturdays off—which was good for morale.

CC: Making a movie on a small budget isn't easy. Did it force you to restrict yourself a lot? Did it feel like a big constraint? Did it help in any way?

PA: One would always like to have more money, but I must say that I enjoyed the challenge of having to make something with very little. It keeps you sharp, on your toes. The film was designed to be small from the start. The previous scripts I'd written for *Smoke* and *Lulu on the Bridge* were quite long—so long that large chunks of filmed material were cut out in the editing room. With *Martin Frost,* I didn't have that luxury. The film was literally edited in the script, so that every scene and every word of dialogue wound up in the finished version of the movie. Not one moment deleted. Tim Squyres, my brilliant, irreplaceable editor (who also cut *Lulu on the Bridge*), edited a big film that came out last year, *Syriana.* He told me they shot over a million feet of film. With *Martin Frost,* we shot about eighty thousand feet—including the slow motion sequences, which eat up film stock at four times the normal rate. The key to pulling off a little film without any resources, I think, is to be prepared. What helped enormously in this case was the rehearsal time I had with the actors before we started shooting. Late last summer, when we were still hopeful that we would begin filming in the fall of '05 in America, Irène came to New York, and the entire cast (with the old Martin) rehearsed for a solid week in Michael Imperioli's sixty-seat theater in Manhattan, Studio Dante. All-day sessions, from early in the morning until late in the afternoon. On two different trips to Paris, I worked alone with Irène at her house for several days at a stretch. Then there were the four days with Irène and David in Lisbon at the beginning of April. And finally, at the end of the month, a full week of rehearsal with the whole cast (except Sophie, who was finishing her freshman year of college) in the house where we shot the film. All this made a big difference. I cut many lines from the script, and by the time we started filming, the actors were truly prepared, comfortable in their roles. For the last day of that rehearsal period, I devised a nutty experiment: we shot the entire film on video—in order, scene by scene. It took about eight hours, and we were all exhausted at the end, but I think it gave us a sense of the film as a whole, and we came up with some new ideas for blocking and camera setups. That was fundamental, but also having a plan when you show up at the set in the morning, a coherent shot list, and an idea of what you want to accomplish during the hours ahead. Paradoxically, the plan gives you the freedom to be spontaneous, the confidence to change things at the last minute.

CC: How do you see the role of director? Is the focus more on transmitting and putting into images your own vision, or is it about coordinating and using the work of an artistic team?

PA: It's both. It has to be both, because in order to get your vision onto the screen, you need the best work possible from the actors, the DP, and the crew. Because the scope of *Martin Frost* was so small, I was personally involved in every aspect of the production. I actually went out shopping for clothes with Adelle, and every picture on the walls of the house, every book on the shelves, every tablecloth and wineglass, I chose with Zé Branco, the production designer. One crazy

Sunday during preproduction, when we were still getting the house ready for the film, I walked into the kitchen and decided that I hated the knobs on the cupboard doors and drawers. They were white porcelain spheres that resembled Ping-Pong balls, and I knew they would look terrible on film—even if you saw them only in the background of a shot. So I unscrewed every damn one of them myself—about fifty or sixty of those hideous Ping-Pong balls—and stashed them away in a drawer.

CC: How do you reconcile what you want with what is being given to you by the actors and the DP?

PA: The director is responsible for everything, and therefore his job is to make every aspect of the film as perfect as possible. If I think something isn't working, we do it again. And again. And again. We keep on doing it until we get it right. Fortunately for me, the actors and the DP on this film were all great artists, and they were as demanding on themselves as I was on myself. There weren't any conflicts. We all kept working until we were happy with the results.

CC: What do you look for in an actor? What is the most important quality?

PA: A good question—and a difficult one to answer. I suppose it begins with a kind of fascination, a desire to watch the person perform. Why do we find some people compelling, while others leave us cold? Why can some actors break our hearts or make us want to laugh our heads off? It's a great mystery to me. How do we know when something is funny or not? If people laugh, it's funny. If they don't laugh, it's not funny. But no comedian has ever known in advance what is going to work or not work. That's why they have to keep trying out their material in front of live audiences. The same with acting. Some people have the gift, others don't. But when you see someone who's really good, you recognize it at once. You're transported, and you can't take your eyes off them.

CC: You collaborated on two films with Wayne Wang, then wrote and directed a film on your own, *Lulu on the Bridge*. Was this experience different—and if so, how?

PA: Some aspects were quite similar, others vastly different. Working with Tim Squyres and Adelle Lutz, for example, a close rapport with the actors, the DP, the crew, the immense pleasure of making a film, the hard work—all that was the same. But *Lulu* was finished eight years ago, and there have been enormous technological changes in filmmaking since then. Not so much with the equipment on the set—we shot *Martin Frost* on thirty-five-millimeter film, the dolly and the dolly tracks were the same, the lights were the same, the boom was the same, and so on—but the way film is processed and edited is very different now. In the old days, you would do a take of a scene, and if you thought it was good, you would say to the script supervisor, "Let's print that one." You don't print anything anymore. The whole day's shooting is digitally scanned from the negative and turned into a DVD. The old ritual of going to a little screening room at the lab every night to watch the rushes is dead. In Portugal, Christophe and I watched the rushes on a TV monitor in my hotel room. And then there are the advances in editing. Tim and I cut *Lulu* on an Avid, which was a fairly big machine in 1998. Now he was able to download the entire Avid program into a laptop, and we've edited the film in my house! That's proved to be a great advantage, since I can smoke my little cigars here while we're working, which keeps me in good spirits. And then, most amazingly, there's the question of the music. Laurent has been composing on a computer in Paris (we'll be recording the music with real musicians in a couple of weeks) and e-mailing the cues to Tim's computer—which we then cut into our digitized version of the film. Luddite that I am, I can only gape. It feels as if we're playing with magic toys.

CC: There are some funny moments in the film. The broken chair, Martin chasing the tire down the road, Fortunato's stories, the outrageous cowboy suit. Yet other scenes are intensely dramatic, or mysterious, at times even mystical. How do you account for these shifts in tone, the oscillation between humor and drama? What role does comedy play in your work—and in *Martin Frost* in particular?

PA: Life is both tragic and funny, both absurd and profoundly meaningful. More or less unconsciously, I've tried to embrace this double aspect of experience in the stories I've written—both novels and screenplays. I feel it's the most honest, most truthful way of looking at the world, and when I think of some of the writers I like best—Shakespeare, Cervantes, Dickens, Kafka, Beckett—they all turn out to be masters of combining the light with the dark, the strange with the familiar. *The Inner Life of Martin Frost* is a very curious story. A story about a man who writes a story about a man who writes a story—and the story inside the story, the film we watch from the moment Martin wakes up to find Claire sleeping beside him to the moment Martin stops typing and looks out the window, is so wild and implausible, so crazy and unpredictable, that without some doses of humor, it would have been unbearably heavy. At the same time, I think the funny bits underscore the pathos of Martin's situation. The tire scene, for example. The viewer knows that Claire has just left the car and run off into the woods, and here comes Martin pushing a tire down the road, unaware that the woman he loves has just disappeared—and suddenly the tire gets away from him. It's classic silent comedy: man versus object. He runs after the tire—only to have it bounce off a stone and knock him to the ground. Funny, but also pathetic. The same goes for Fortunato, with all his weird comments, bad jokes, and ridiculous short stories. He shows up when Martin is at his most abject, suffering over the loss of Claire, and amusing as I find this character to be, his presence underscores the powerful loneliness that has enveloped Martin. The saddest scene in the film is also one of the funniest: when Martin practices Screwdriver Darts on his own. The poor man is so lost, he doesn't know what to do with himself anymore.

CC: Screwdriver Darts. Where did you come up with that idea?

PA: The inspiration came from something that happened in my childhood. I was ten or eleven years old, and one day after school I went back to the house of my best friend. For some reason, he had decided to set up his bedroom in the basement, and there we were, sitting in that room, which had soft, knotty pine walls, throwing a screwdriver and trying to get it to stick in the wood. Don't ask me why we were doing it. That's all I remember. Throwing the screwdriver and trying to get it to stick in the wood. Neither one of us could do it. We threw the screwdriver ten times, twenty times, thirty times, with no success at all. Then my friend's older brother came downstairs and poked his head in the door. He must have been about fourteen and was much bigger and stronger than we were. "What are you two idiots up to?" he asked. We explained that we were trying to get the screwdriver to stick in the wall, but it couldn't be done, it was physically impossible. "Of course it's possible," my friend's brother said. "Do you want to bet?" Naturally we wanted to bet, since we were convinced we would win. The stakes were set at five dollars, a tremendous amount of money for kids back then, the equivalent of ten or twenty weeks' allowance. We gave the screwdriver to the brother, who was still standing by the door, and without even pausing to think, he raised the thing behind his head and let off a fiendishly powerful throw. The screwdriver sailed clear across the room, and then bang, it stuck in the wall. It left an indelible impression on me. And that was how Screwdriver Darts was born. I'm hoping it will catch on after the movie comes out and that Screwdriver Dart leagues will be set up all around the world.

CC: The pivotal scene in the film is when Claire dies and Martin brings her back to life by burning the pages of his story. Do you think writing is a dangerous weapon? Can it kill?

PA: Writing can certainly be dangerous. Dangerous for the reader—if something is powerful enough to change his view of the world—and dangerous for the writer. Think of how many writers were murdered by Stalin: Osip Mandelstam, Isaac Babel, untold others. Think of the fatwa against Salman Rushdie. Think of all the imprisoned writers in the world today. But can writing kill? No, not literally. A book isn't a machine gun or an electric chair. And yet, strange things sometimes happen that make you stop and wonder. The case of the French writer Louis-René des Forêts, for instance. I first heard about it when I was living in Paris in the early seventies, and it haunted me so much that I wound up incorporating it into one of my novels years later, *Oracle Night*. Des Forêts was a promising young writer in the fifties who had published one novel and one collection of stories. Then he wrote a narrative poem in which a child drowns in the sea. Not long after the book was published, his own child drowned. There might not have been any rational link between the imaginary death and the real death, but des Forêts was so shattered by the experience that he stopped writing for decades. A terrible story. It's not hard to understand how he felt.

CC: *The Inner Life of Martin Frost* begins with a slow tracking shot of a series of family photographs. If one looks closely, one recognizes that these are pictures of you and your wife, Siri Hustvedt. Supposedly, these two people are the owners of the house, Jack and Diane Restau, Martin's friends. If you rearrange the letters of the name *Restau*, it becomes *Auster*. Immediately after we see the photographs, the camera stops in front of the door, and an unseen narrator begins to speak. The name of the narrator is not credited in the film, but the voice happens to belong to you. Would you care to explain?

PA: When I thought about what we would need to make the house look like a real house lived in by real people, family photos were among the first things that sprang to mind. Every family has photos scattered around the house. Rather than go to the expense of taking pictures of actors, I pulled forty or fifty photos from our own albums and took them to Portugal with me. Why not? They were authentic family pictures, and if someone recognized Siri and me, fine. If they didn't, that was fine, too. As for the name *Restau* and the fact that I did the narration myself, I think they add a subtle but interesting element to the film—for those who figure out the scrambled name or recognize my voice. Everyone who sees the film will know from the credits that I'm the writer and the director. I'm the man who wrote the story about the man who wrote the story about the man who wrote the story. Why pretend otherwise?

*August 22, 2006*

# the inner life
# of martin frost

Written and Directed by
**Paul Auster**

Produced by
**Paulo Branco, Paul Auster, Yael Melalede**

Director of Photography
**Christophe Beaucarne**

Editor
**Tim Squyres**

Production Designer
**Zé Branco**

Costumes
**Adelle Lutz**

Music
**Laurent Petitgand**

Executive Producers
**Peter Newman, Greg Johnson, Eva Kolodner**

# CAST
*(In order of appearance)*

| | |
|---|---|
| Martin Frost | **David Thewlis** |
| Claire Martin | **Irène Jacob** |
| James Fortunato | **Michael Imperioli** |
| Anna James | **Sophie Auster** |

## 1. INT. A COUNTRY HOUSE—DAY

*A slow, methodical tracking shot through the ground floor of a country house. The camera skims along the walls, floats above the furniture in the living room, and eventually comes to a stop eight feet from the door in the entrance hall.*

> NARRATOR (*voice-over*)

The house was empty.

*The door opens, and in walks* MARTIN FROST, *a man in his early forties. He is carrying a suitcase in one hand and a bag of groceries in the other. As he kicks the door shut behind him, the voice-over narration continues.*

> NARRATOR (*voice-over*)

His friends Jack and Diane Restau were going to be gone until the end of the year. If Martin felt like getting out of New York for a while, Jack said, he could camp out at their place any time he wanted.

MARTIN *puts down the suitcase and then exits the frame with the grocery bag.*

> NARRATOR (*voice-over*)

Martin had just spent three years writing a novel, and his brain was tired, in need of a rest. He had no plans. All he wanted was to spend a couple of weeks in the country and do nothing, to live the life of a stone.

As we listen to the NARRATOR's voice, we see MARTIN wandering around in various parts of the house. He carries the groceries into the kitchen, but the moment the bag touches the counter, the scene cuts to the living room, where we find him inspecting the books on the shelves. As his hand reaches for one of the books, we jump to the master bedroom, where MARTIN is opening and closing the drawers of the bureau, putting away his things. A drawer bangs shut, and an instant later he is sitting on the bed, testing the bounce of the mattress.

It is a jagged montage, combining close and medium shots in a succession of slightly off-kilter angles and cuts paced at varied, unexpected tempos.

The camera fixes on the photograph of a young girl. As we listen to the last words of the opening monologue ("to live the life of a stone"), the image begins to blur. Silence follows. For a beat or two, it is as if everything has stopped—the voice, the sounds, the images—and then, very abruptly, the scene shifts. Cut to:


## 2. EXT. THE GROUNDS OF THE HOUSE—DAY

MARTIN is walking in the garden. A long shot is followed by a close shot; MARTIN's face, and then a languid perusal of the things around him: trees and shrubs, the sky. When the camera finds him again, MARTIN is crouching down to observe a procession of ants. We hear the wind rush through the trees—a prolonged sibilance, roaring like the sound of surf. MARTIN looks up, shielding his eyes from the sun, and again we cut away from him to another part of the landscape: MARTIN is walking slowly, deep in thought. He approaches the camera and then exits the frame. Meanwhile:

NARRATOR (voice-over)

But what did he know? A few hours of silence, a few gulps of fresh air, and all of a sudden an idea for a story was turning around in his head. That's how it always seems to work with stories. One minute there's nothing. And the next minute it's there, already sitting inside you.

*A wide shot of the trees. The wind is blowing again, and as the leaves and branches tremble under the assault, the sound amplifies into a pulsing, breathlike wave of percussiveness, an airborne clamor of sighs. Then, once again, the scene shifts abruptly. Cut to:*

## 3. INT. THE HOUSE HALLWAY—DAY

*MARTIN walks down the hall and opens a closet door. He looks inside, immediately shuts the door, and then opens the next door. He reaches in and pulls out a fifty-year-old Olympia typewriter. Shutting the door behind him, he carries the typewriter into a small study across the hall.*

## 4. INT. THE STUDY—DAY

*MARTIN is sitting at the desk with the typewriter in front of him. After a moment, he begins examining the contents of the drawers. The first drawer is empty; he slams it shut. In the second drawer he finds some ballpoint pens, some pencils, and a pad of yellow legal paper. One by one, he puts these items on the desk, then slams the drawer shut. In the third drawer he discovers a stack of blank white paper—about two hundred sheets. He pulls out the whole stack and puts it on the desk beside the typewriter, then slams the drawer shut. A brief pause as he surveys the objects in front of him. After a moment, he begins to arrange them: centering the typewriter on the surface of the desk, aligning the paper, putting the pens and pencils in a neat, orderly row. Finally, he removes the top sheet of paper and rolls it into the machine. He begins typing.*

NARRATOR (*voice-over*)

It might not have been the newest equipment in the world. But it worked.

*Close-up of the sheet in the typewriter. We can read: "It might not be the newest equipment in the world . . . but it works." Cut to:*

## 5. INT. MASTER BEDROOM—NIGHT

*MARTIN is lying in bed with his eyes open. The bedside lamp is on.*

NARRATOR (*voice-over*)

It wasn't going to be a long story. Twenty-five or thirty pages, forty at the most. Martin didn't know how much time he would need to write it, but he decided to stay in the house until it was finished.

*MARTIN leans over and turns out the light. Darkness.*

NARRATOR (*voice-over*)

That was the new plan. He would write the story, and he wouldn't leave until it was finished.

## 6. EXT. THE GROUNDS OF THE HOUSE—DAY

*A close shot of a leaf, trembling in the light, followed by a close shot of wild-flowers jutting up from the grass in the garden. Early morning.*

## 7. INT. MASTER BEDROOM—DAY

*A tight shot of* MARTIN'*s face shows him to be asleep, his head resting on a pillow. Sunlight pours through the slatted shutters, and as we watch him open his eyes and struggle to wake up, the camera pulls back to reveal something that cannot be true, that defies the laws of common sense.* MARTIN *has not spent the night alone. There is a young woman in bed with him,* CLAIRE MARTIN.

*As the camera continues dollying back into the room, we see that she is asleep under the covers, curled up on her side and turned toward* MARTIN*—her left arm flung casually across his chest. As* MARTIN *gradually emerges from his torpor, he notices the bare arm lying across his chest, then realizes that the arm is attached to a body, and then sits up in bed, looking like someone who's just been given an electric shock.*

*Jostled by these sudden movements,* CLAIRE *groans, buries her head in the pillow, and then opens her eyes. At first, she doesn't notice that* MARTIN *is there. Still groggy, still fighting her way into consciousness, she rolls onto her back and yawns. As her arms stretch out, her right hand brushes against* MARTIN'*s body. Nothing happens for a second or two, and then, very slowly, she sits up, looks into* MARTIN'*s confused and horrified face, and shrieks. An instant later, she flings back the covers and bounds from the bed, rushing across the room in a frenzy of fear and embarrassment. She is dressed in nearly nothing—at most a skimpy, sleeveless T-shirt. She snatches her bathrobe from the back of a chair and hastily thrusts her arms into the sleeves.*

MARTIN
(*Beside himself*) Who are you? What are you doing here?

CLAIRE
(*Equally beside herself*) No—who are *you*? And what are *you* doing here?

MARTIN

(*Incredulous*) Me?

*He climbs out of bed, picks up his pants from the floor, puts them over his boxer shorts, and begins walking toward* CLAIRE. *She grows increasingly frightened—but holds her ground.*

CLAIRE

(*Raising her hand*) Uh-uh-uh. That's close enough.

MARTIN

(*Angry*) I'm Martin Frost—not that it's any of your business—and unless you tell me who you are right now, I'm going to call the police.

CLAIRE

(*Astonished*) You're Martin Frost? The real Martin Frost?

MARTIN

(*Angrier still*) That's what I just said. Do I have to say it again?

CLAIRE

(*Flustered; talking rapidly*) It's just that I know you, that's all. Not that I really know you, but I know who you are. You're Martin Frost the writer. Jack and Diane's friend.

MARTIN

You know Jack and Diane?

CLAIRE

I'm Diane's niece.

MARTIN

(*Beat; absorbing this information*) What's your name?

CLAIRE

Claire.

MARTIN

Claire what?

CLAIRE

Claire . . . (*Hesitates*) . . . Martin.

MARTIN

(*Snorts with disgust*) What is this, some kind of joke?

CLAIRE

I can't help it. That's my name.

MARTIN

And what are you doing here, Claire *Martin*?

CLAIRE

Diane invited me. (*Beat. She reaches for her purse, which is lying on the chair*) Look, if you don't believe me . . . (*She opens the purse, fumbles through it. Finally, she pulls out a key and holds it up to Martin*) You see? Diane gave it to me. It's the key to the front door.

MARTIN

(*Digs into his pocket and pulls out an identical key. He holds it up to her, jabbing it right under her nose*) Then why would Jack give me this one?

CLAIRE

Because . . . (*Backing away from him*) . . . because he's Jack, that's why. I mean, you know them. He and Diane are always doing things like that.

*MARTIN is defeated. Understanding that CLAIRE has just as much right to be in the house as he does, he turns away from her and begins pacing around the room.*

MARTIN

I don't like it. I came here to be alone. I have work to do, and having you around is . . . is . . . well, it's not being alone, is it?

CLAIRE

Don't worry. I won't get in your way. I'm here to work on my thesis.

*MARTIN sits down on the edge of the bed and lets out a sigh.*

CLAIRE (*cont'd*)

I have a lot of reading to do.

MARTIN

(*Staring down at the floor*) Reading is bad for your health.

CLAIRE

Only high-cholesterol books. I read low-fat, vegetarian stuff.

MARTIN

What's your field? The history of the boiled turnip?

CLAIRE

Philosophy.

MARTIN

(*Muttering under his breath*) Philosophy. (*Beat*) Chewy, but not much taste.

CLAIRE

This week I'll be reading Bishop Berkeley. (*Pronounces the name "Bark-lee"*)

MARTIN

If a tree falls in a forest and no one hears it, does it make a sound or not?

CLAIRE

More like: Is the tree really there? Berkeley's the one who said that matter doesn't exist. That everything is in our head.

MARTIN

But you're not in my head, are you? You exist, and I have to share this house with you.

CLAIRE

I'll be very quiet, I promise. I'll move my things into another bedroom, and you won't even know I'm here.

MARTIN

(*Accepting total defeat; slaps his knees and stands up*) Okay. You stay out of my way, and I'll stay out of yours. Deal?

CLAIRE

If that's what you want, that's how it will be.

MARTIN

Good. (*Starts to leave*) I'm going to work now. See you later.

CLAIRE

(*Amused*) But you just said you *didn't* want to see me.

(*Stops*) A figure of speech. It means good-bye. (*Beat*) Good-bye. (*He begins walking again*)

*As* MARTIN *exits the frame, the camera swings around and slowly pushes in on* CLAIRE'S *face. It is our first serious look at her in repose, and it should achieve the effect of a visual caress. She follows* MARTIN *with her eyes, watching him as he leaves the room, and an instant after the camera comes to a halt in front of her, we hear the latch of the door click shut. The expression on* CLAIRE'S *face doesn't change.*

CLAIRE

(*Barely above a whisper*) Good-bye, Martin.

## 8. INT. THE STUDY—DAY

*Later that morning.* MARTIN *is sitting at the desk, typing.*

## 9. EXT. THE GROUNDS OF THE HOUSE—DAY

CLAIRE *is sitting on the grass under a tree, reading* The Principles of Human Knowledge *by George Berkeley. The sounds of* MARTIN'S *typewriter can be heard faintly in the distance.* CLAIRE *is wearing blue jeans and a T-shirt with a single word written across the front:* BERKELEY. *She reads the text out loud to herself in a low voice.*

CLAIRE

"And it seems to me no less evident that the various sensations or ideas imprinted on the sense, however blended or combined together, cannot exist otherwise than in a mind perceiving them."

## 10. INT. THE STUDY—DAY

*As before:* MARTIN *sitting at his desk, typing. He comes to the bottom of a page, pulls it out of the typewriter, and then rolls in another sheet of paper.*

## 11. EXT. THE GROUNDS OF THE HOUSE—DAY

*As before:* CLAIRE *reading Berkeley.*

> CLAIRE
> "Secondly, it will be objected that there is a great difference betwixt real fire and the idea of fire, between dreaming or imagining oneself burnt, and actually being so."

## 12. EXT. THE STUDY—DAY

*As before:* MARTIN *sitting at his desk. This time he is correcting his typed pages with a pencil. Eventually, he puts the finished pages in a drawer and then swivels in his chair to look out the window.*

## 13. EXT. THE GROUNDS OF THE HOUSE—DAY

*As before:* CLAIRE *reading Berkeley, in silence.* MARTIN *enters the frame with his back to the camera.* CLAIRE *looks up.*

> CLAIRE
> Hello.

MARTIN

(*Stiff; bumbling; awkward*) I'm sorry. I wasn't very nice to you this morning. I shouldn't have acted that way.

*CLAIRE smiles, accepting MARTIN's embarrassed apology. A brief pause.*

CLAIRE

What time is it?

CLAIRE

A little after six.

CLAIRE

(*Holding up her book*) I have one more section to go. Why don't we meet up in the living room in about half an hour and have a drink?

MARTIN

Good idea. As long as we're stuck with each other, we might as well act like civilized people.

## 14. INT. THE LIVING ROOM—NIGHT

*MARTIN and CLAIRE are sitting side by side on a large sofa, drinking red wine. The bottle is on a coffee table in front of them, half-empty.*

MARTIN

(*Reaching for the bottle*) A little more?

CLAIRE

Yes, please.

*He pours wine into her glass, then refills his own glass as well.*

MARTIN

(*Putting the bottle on the table*) Are you wearing that shirt because you're reading Berkeley this week? (*He pronounces the word "Bark-lee"*) Do you have another one for next week that says "Hume"?

CLAIRE

(*Laughs*) No, no. (*Pointing to her T-shirt*) This says "*Berk*-lee." The philosopher I'm reading is *Bark*-lee. The words are pronounced differently.

MARTIN

It's the same spelling. Therefore, it's the same word.

CLAIRE

It's the same spelling, but it's two different words.

MARTIN

Are you trying to confuse me?

CLAIRE

(*Taking a big sip of wine*) You should talk, Mr. Frost. You once wrote a story about two characters with the same name.

*She holds out her glass to* MARTIN, *who obliges by picking up the bottle and pouring her more wine.* CLAIRE *immediately takes another sip.*

MARTIN

(*Surprised*) So you read that story. You must be one of six people in the universe who knows about it. It was published in a little magazine more than fifteen years ago.

CLAIRE

I've read everything you've written. All four novels and the two plays.

MARTIN

But I've published only three novels.


CLAIRE

You've just finished a new one, haven't you? You gave a copy of the manuscript to Diane and Jack. Diane lent it to me, and I read it last week. (*Beat*) I think it's the best thing you've done.


*By now, whatever reservations* MARTIN *might have had about* CLAIRE *have all but melted away. Not only is she a spirited and intelligent person, not only is she exceedingly pleasant to look at, but she knows and admires his work. He pours himself another glass of wine, leans back in his seat, and smiles. It is the first time since the opening of the film that the brooding, ever serious* MARTIN FROST *has let down his guard.*


MARTIN

In other words, Miss Martin approves.


CLAIRE

Oh yes, most definitely.


MARTIN

Miss Martin approves of Martin.


CLAIRE

Yes, Martin. Miss Martin approves of Martin.


MARTIN

And reads Bark-lee at Berk-lee. Or is it Berk-lee at Bark-lee? (*Beat*) What does that T-shirt say again? Is it the man or the college?


CLAIRE

It's both. It says whatever you want it to say.

*A small glint of mischief flashes in* CLAIRE's *eyes. Something has occurred to her—a thought, an impulse, a sudden inspiration. She puts her glass on the table and stands up.*

CLAIRE *(cont'd)*

Or . . . it doesn't mean anything at all.

*By way of demonstration, she peels off the T-shirt and calmly tosses it on the floor. She is wearing a lacy black bra—hardly the kind of garment one would expect to discover on such an earnest student of ideas. But this is an idea, too, of course, and now that she has put it into action with such a bold and decisive gesture,* MARTIN *can only gape.*

MARTIN

*(Trying to absorb what has just happened)* Well, that's one way of eliminating the confusion.

CLAIRE

*(Smiling)* Simple logic.

MARTIN

*(A long pause; studying her)* And yet, by eliminating one kind of confusion, you only create another.

CLAIRE

Don't be confused, Martin. I'm trying to be as clear as I can.

MARTIN

Claire is clear. *(Another pause; studying her)* And Claire is cute.

CLAIRE

*(Grinning back at him)* You think so?

Oh yes, most definitely.

*Cut to:*


## 15. INT. MASTER BEDROOM—NIGHT

*CLAIRE and MARTIN come crashing into the dimly lit bedroom. They are walking and embracing at the same time, stumbling sideways with their arms around each other and their mouths locked in a prolonged kiss. Sudden grunts, rapid breaths, aroused whimpers. They fall on top of the bed, still holding on to each other, and begin to tug and tear at each other's clothes.*

*Fade out.*


## 16. INT. ANYWHERE

*The screen remains black for four seconds. Silence.*

*A puff of cigarette smoke wafts into the frame. As it breaks apart and swirls before our eyes, we hear:*

NARRATOR (*voice-over*)
Every story has a shape . . .

*Cut to:*


## 17. INT. THE KITCHEN—DAY

*A close-up of a kettle on the stove. Steam is pouring from the spout.*

NARRATOR (*voice-over*)

. . . and the shape of every story is different . . .

*Cut to:*


## 18. INT SPARE BEDROOM—DAY

*A medium shot of a pair of thin white curtains fluttering in the embrasure of a half-open window.*

NARRATOR (*voice-over*)

. . . from the shape of every other story.

*Cut to:*


## 19. EXT. OUTSIDE THE HOUSE—DAY

*A wide shot of the back of the house.*

*The camera moves in on the window of the study. We see* MARTIN *at his desk, correcting pages of his manuscript with a pencil. Cut to:*

*A similar shot of* CLAIRE *through the living room window. We see her sitting on the sofa reading* A Treatise of Human Nature, *by David Hume.*

*Meanwhile, the narration continues.*

NARRATOR (*voice-over*)

Some stories move in straight lines. Others make circles . . . or zigzags . . . or pirouettes.

*Cut to:*

## 20. INT. THE STUDY—DAY

*As we listen to the* NARRATOR's *voice, we see* MARTIN *kneeling on the floor of the study with a red T-shirt spread out before him. Working with a paint-brush and a can of white paint, he carefully writes the following letters across the front of the shirt: H-U-M-E.*

NARRATOR (*voice-over*)

Rather than go in one general direction, Martin's story seemed to be looping back around itself—or veering off in a series of sharp right-angle turns—or spiraling in toward some invisible point at the center. (*Beat*) Like this, maybe.

*Cut to:*

## 21. INT. ANYWHERE

*To be filmed in a stop-action sequence that will create the effect of animation. Against a blank white screen, a drawing takes shape before our eyes:*

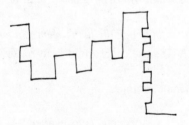

NARRATOR (*voice-over*)

Or this.

*Another stop-action drawing:*

*Cut to:*

## 22. INT. THE LIVING ROOM—DAY

*As the narration continues, MARTIN enters the living room and presents the "Hume" T-shirt to CLAIRE. She is delighted. Standing up from the sofa, she pulls off her Berkeley T-shirt (revealing a lacy red bra underneath) and puts on the new one. She does a small, sprightly turn, modeling her gift for MARTIN. Then, unexpectedly, she immediately pulls it off and opens her arms. MARTIN enters her embrace, and they begin to kiss.*

NARRATOR (voice-over)

Whatever the story looked like, Martin was doing it, and every day he was getting a little farther with it, understanding it a little better, and every day he added a few more pages to the pile.

*Still kissing CLAIRE, MARTIN unhooks the clasp of her bra. She steps back for a moment, tosses the garment aside, and begins to unbutton MARTIN's shirt.*

*Fade out.*

## 23. EXT. NEAR THE SWIMMING POOL—DAY

*We hear* CLAIRE *and* MARTIN *laughing. The camera, traveling slowly through the garden, discovers them sitting at a table, finishing off a Sunday brunch.* CLAIRE *is wearing her Hume T-shirt.*

MARTIN

And then I said to him, If you don't believe me, I'll show you. And then I reached into my pocket and—

*At that moment a cell phone rings, and* MARTIN *stops in the middle of his story. As* CLAIRE *and* MARTIN *talk, the telephone continues to ring.*

MARTIN

(*Playing dumb*) What's that?

CLAIRE

(*In the same spirit*) What's what?

MARTIN

That noise. Don't you hear it?

CLAIRE

Oh, *that.* (*Beat*) Yes, I hear it.

MARTIN

A kind of ringing, wouldn't you say?

CLAIRE

A ringing. Or maybe a kind of . . . tinkling.

MARTIN

Sounds like the outside world to me.

You mean there are other people besides us?

*MARTIN pulls the phone out of his pocket.*

MARTIN

I don't think so. It must be an illusion. (*Pushes the answer button on the phone*) Hello. (*Listens*) Jack! How are you? (*Covers the receiver with his hand and whispers to* CLAIRE) Jack and Diane.

*CLAIRE's expression changes from one of joyful camaraderie to concern, perhaps even alarm.*

MARTIN (*cont'd*)

Calcutta! (*Covers the receiver with his hand and whispers to* CLAIRE) They're in Calcutta.

*CLAIRE looks increasingly upset.*

MARTIN (*cont'd*)

(*Listens*) The boiler. Diane's worried about the boiler. (*Listens*) Okay. (*Listens*) If anything goes wrong, I call Jim Fortunato. Fortunato Plumbing and Heat. (*Listens*) I got it. Okay. (*Listens*) Anyway, it's a good thing you called.

*CLAIRE stands up and begins to walk away from the table.*

MARTIN (*cont'd*)

Claire and I were just discussing whether you were real or not. What should I tell her?

*CLAIRE, in great distress, walks quickly across the grass.*

MARTIN *(cont'd)*

*(Confused by* CLAIRE's *behavior; goes on listening)* What do you mean, "Who's Claire?" Claire Martin. Diane's niece. *(Listens; utterly astonished)* What?

*Cut to:*

## 24. EXT. NEAR THE SWIMMING POOL—DAY

MARTIN *stands up from the table and runs across the grass.*

MARTIN

*(Shouting)* Claire!

*He exits the frame. Cut to:*

## 25. EXT. THE GROUNDS OF THE HOUSE—DAY

*A medium shot of* CLAIRE, *from behind, running away.* MARTIN *enters the frame and catches up to her. Reaching out and grabbing her elbow, he spins her around and forces her to stop. They are both out of breath. Chests heaving, lungs gasping for air, neither one of them able to talk.*

*At last.*

MARTIN

What's going on, Claire? Tell me, what's going on?

CLAIRE *doesn't answer.*

MARTIN *(cont'd)*
*(Leaning forward and shouting in her face)* You have to tell me!

CLAIRE
*(In a calm voice)* I can hear you. You don't have to shout, Martin.

MARTIN
I've just been told that Diane has one sister. She has two children, and both of them happen to be boys. That makes two nephews, Claire, but no niece.

CLAIRE
I didn't know what else to do. I had to find a way to make you trust me. After a day or two, I thought you'd figure it out on your own— and then it wouldn't matter anymore.

MARTIN
Figure out what?

*Until now, CLAIRE has looked embarrassed, more or less contrite, not so much ashamed of her deception as disappointed that she has been found out. Once MARTIN confesses to his ignorance, however, the look changes. She is genuinely surprised.*

CLAIRE
Don't you get it, Martin? We've been together for almost a week, and you're telling me you still don't get it?

*It goes without saying that he doesn't. The bright and beautiful CLAIRE has turned into an enigma, and the more she says, the less MARTIN is able to follow her.*

MARTIN

Who are you? What the hell are you doing here?


CLAIRE

(*Suddenly on the verge of tears*) Oh, Martin. It doesn't matter who I am.


MARTIN

Of course it does. It matters very much.

*A close-up of* CLAIRE's *face.*


CLAIRE

No, my darling, it doesn't.


MARTIN

How can you say that?


CLAIRE

It doesn't matter because you love me. Because you want me. *That's* what matters. All the rest is nothing.

*Fade out.*


## 26. INT. THE STUDY—DAY

*The screen remains black for several seconds. A slow fade-in begins, and as the new image settles into focus, the entire screen is filled with an immense, tightly framed shot of* MARTIN's *eyes.*

*The camera holds in that position for two or three beats, and then, as the voice-over narration begins, it starts to pull back, revealing* MARTIN's *face,* MARTIN's *shoulders, and finally* MARTIN *sitting at the desk. He looks down at the type-writer with a pensive expression.*

> NARRATOR (*voice-over*)
> Unfortunately, Claire was right. Martin did love her, and he did want her. But how can you love someone you don't trust?

*With no halt in its backward progress, the camera leaves the room . . .*

*Dissolve to:*

## 27. INT. MASTER BEDROOM—NIGHT

*. . . and we are inside, moving in on* CLAIRE *as she sits in front of a dressing table mirror applying makeup to her face. She has nothing on but a black bra and panties.*

*Eyebrow pencil, mascara, cheek rouge, powder, lipstick.* CLAIRE *goes on working in front of the mirror, transforming herself from one kind of a woman into another. The impulsive tomboy disappears, and in her place emerges a glamorous, sophisticated, movie-star temptress.* CLAIRE *stands up from the table and wriggles into a narrow black cocktail dress, slips her feet into a pair of three-inch heels, and we scarcely recognize her anymore. She cuts a ravishing figure: self-possessed, confident, the very picture of feminine power. With the trace of a smile on her lips, she checks herself in the mirror one last time and then walks out of the room. Dissolve to:*

## 28. INT. THE UPSTAIRS HALLWAY—NIGHT

CLAIRE *walks down the hall and stops in front of the door of* MARTIN*'s study. She knocks.*

The food is ready, Martin. I'll be waiting for you in the dining room.

*Cut to:*

## 29. INT. THE DINING ROOM—NIGHT

*CLAIRE is sitting at the table, calmly waiting for MARTIN. She has already set out the appetizers (asparagus vinaigrette with lemon wedges); the wine has been uncorked; the candles have been lit.*

*MARTIN enters the room in silence. CLAIRE greets him with a warm, friendly smile, but MARTIN pays no attention to it. He seems wary, out of sorts, not at all sure of how he should act.*

*Eyeing CLAIRE with suspicion, he walks over to the place that has been set for him, pulls out the chair, and begins to sit down. The chair appears to be solid, but no sooner does he lower his weight onto it than it splinters into a dozen pieces. MARTIN goes tumbling to the floor.*

CLAIRE

Are you okay?

*It is a wholly unexpected turn of events. CLAIRE bursts out laughing, but MARTIN is not at all amused. Sprawled out on his rear end, he smolders in a funk of injured pride and resentment, and the longer CLAIRE goes on laughing at him (she can't help herself; it's simply too funny), the more ridiculous he is made to look. Without saying a word, MARTIN slowly climbs to his feet, kicks aside the bits of broken chair, and puts another chair in its place. He sits down cautiously this time, and when he is at last assured that the seat is strong enough to hold him, he turns his attention to the food.*

MARTIN

(*Trying to maintain his dignity; subdued*) Looks good.


CLAIRE

(*Smiling; inordinately pleased by the comment*) And so, Martin, how's your story going?


*Refusing to answer CLAIRE's question, he leans forward and looks her straight in the eye.*


MARTIN

(*Intensely*) Who are you, Claire? What are you doing here?


CLAIRE

(*Unruffled; smiling back at him*) No, you answer my question first. How's your story going?


*MARTIN looks as if he's about to snap. Maddened by her evasions, he just stares at her and says nothing.*


CLAIRE (*cont'd*)

Please, Martin. It's very important.


MARTIN

(*Struggling to control his temper*) You really want to know?


CLAIRE

Yes, I really want to know.


MARTIN

All right . . . All right, I'll tell you how it's going. It's . . . (*Reflects for a moment*) It's . . . (*Continuing to think*) Actually . . . it's going quite well.

CLAIRE

Quite well . . . or very well?


MARTIN

Um . . . (*Thinking*) . . . very well. I'd say it's going very well.


CLAIRE

(*With a broad, satisfied smile*) You see?


MARTIN

See what?


CLAIRE

Oh, Martin. Of course you do.


MARTIN

No, Claire, I don't. I don't see anything. If you want to know the truth, I'm completely lost.


CLAIRE

Poor Martin. You shouldn't be so hard on yourself.


*MARTIN gives her a lame smile. They have reached a kind of standoff, and for the moment there is nothing more to be said. CLAIRE digs into her food. She eats with obvious enjoyment, savoring the taste of her concoction with small, tentative bites.*


CLAIRE

Mmm. (*Chews*) Not bad. What do you think, Martin?


*MARTIN lifts his fork to take a bite, but just as he is about to put the food in his mouth, he glances over at CLAIRE, distracted by the soft moans of pleasure emanating from her throat, and with his attention briefly diverted from the*

*matter at hand, his wrist turns downward by a few degrees. As the fork contin-*
*ues its journey toward his mouth, a thin trail of vinaigrette sauce comes drip-*
*ping off the utensil and slides down the front of his shirt. At first, MARTIN*
*doesn't notice, but as his mouth opens and his eyes return to the looming*
*morsel of asparagus, he suddenly sees what is happening. He jumps back and*
*lets go of the fork.*

                              MARTIN
Christ! I've done it again!

*Suddenly understanding that he is powerless against CLAIRE's charms, MAR-*
*TIN turns to her and smiles.*

*The camera cuts to CLAIRE (who bursts out laughing for the second time) and*
*then dollies in on her for a close-up.*

*The shot is similar to the one that ended the scene in the bedroom at the be-*
*ginning of the film, but whereas CLAIRE's face was motionless as she watched*
*MARTIN make his exit, now it is animated, brimming with delight, express-*
*ing what seems to be an almost transcendent joy. For a few seconds, CLAIRE*
*is turned into something indestructible, an embodiment of pure human ra-*
*diance.*

*Then the picture begins to dissolve, breaking apart against a background of solid*
*blackness, and although CLAIRE's laughter goes on for several more seconds, it*
*begins to break apart as well—fading into a series of echoes, of disjointed breaths,*
*of ever more distant reverberations. Cut to:*

## 30. EXT. ANYWHERE—NIGHT

*Silence. The screen is dominated by a single image: MARTIN's typewriter, re-*
*volving slowly in black limbo.*

That night, Martin made one of the most important decisions of his life. He decided that he wasn't going to raise any more questions. Claire was asking him to make a leap of faith, and rather than go on pressing her, he decided to close his eyes and jump. He had no idea what was waiting for him at the bottom, but that didn't mean it wasn't worth the risk. And so he kept on falling . . . and a week later, just when he was beginning to think nothing could ever go wrong, Claire went out for a walk.

## 31. INT. THE STUDY—DAY

*MARTIN is sitting at his desk. He turns from the typewriter to look out the window, and as the angle reverses to register his point of view, we see a long shot of CLAIRE walking alone in the garden. A cold front has apparently arrived. She is wearing a scarf and overcoat, and her hands are in her pockets.*

*CLAIRE takes a few more steps, and then, without warning, she collapses to the ground. No tottering or dizziness, no gradual buckling of the knees. Between one step and the next, CLAIRE plunges into total unconsciousness, and from the sudden, merciless way her strength gives out on her, it looks as if she's dead. Cut to:*

## 32. EXT. THE GARDEN—MOMENTS LATER

*A long shot of the inert, recumbent CLAIRE.*

*MARTIN enters the frame: running, out of breath, frantic. He falls to his knees and cradles her head in his hands, looking for a sign of life. CLAIRE eventually opens her eyes, but enough time elapses for us to know that it isn't a recovery so much as a stay of execution, an augur of things to come. She looks up at MARTIN and smiles. It is a spiritual smile somehow, an inward smile, the smile of someone who no longer believes in the future.* MARTIN *kisses her, and then he bends down, gathers* CLAIRE *into his arms, and begins carrying her toward the house.*

NARRATOR (*voice-over*)

(*From the moment Claire opens her eyes*) She seemed to be all right. Just a little fainting spell, they thought. But the next morning, Claire woke up with a high fever.


## 33. INT. MASTER BEDROOM—DAY

*As the narration continues, we see* CLAIRE *lying in bed. Hovering around her like a nurse,* MARTIN *takes her temperature and plies her with aspirin.*

NARRATOR (*voice-over*)

She didn't complain. Her skin was hot to the touch, but she seemed to be in good spirits. After a while, she pushed Martin out of the room, insisting that he go back to his story.


## 34. INT. THE STUDY—DAY

MARTIN *is sitting at the desk, typing another page of his story. The sound is particularly intense here—keys clattering at a furious rhythm, great staccato bursts of activity—but then the volume diminishes, falls off into near silence, and the* NARRATOR's *voice returns. Cut to:*


## 35. INT. MASTER BEDROOM—DAY

*One by one, we see a succession of highly detailed close-ups, still-life render-ings of the tiny world around* CLAIRE's *sickbed: a glass of water, the edge of a closed book, a thermometer, glimpses of* CLAIRE's *arm and neck and hands.*

NARRATOR (*voice-over*)

The next morning, the fever was worse. Martin told her he was taking the day off, whether she liked it or not. He sat beside her for several hours, and by the middle of the afternoon she seemed to take a turn for the better. The fever broke, and suddenly she was back to her old self.

*The camera jumps back to a wide shot of the room, and there she is, sitting up in bed, looking perfectly well. In a mock serious voice, she is reading a passage from Kant's* Critique of Pure Reason *out loud to* MARTIN.

CLAIRE

". . . things which we see are not by themselves what we see . . . so that, if we drop our subject or the subjective form of our senses, all qualities, all relations of objects in space and time, nay space and time themselves, would vanish."

*Cut to:*


## 36. INT. THE KITCHEN—DAY

*The next morning.* MARTIN *is preparing breakfast in the kitchen.*

*He puts the meal on a tray and leaves the room.*

NARRATOR (*voice-over*)

Martin felt encouraged . . .

*Cut to:*


## 37. INT. MASTER BEDROOM—DAY

*A fire is burning in the fireplace.*

*MARTIN enters the bedroom with the tray. CLAIRE, who is sitting up in bed reading Kant, gives him a warm smile.*

> NARRATOR (*voice-over*)
>
> . . . and the next day he returned to his story.

*He puts the tray on the bed and kisses CLAIRE, but before he can sit down and settle in, she shoos him out of the room.*


## 38. INT. THE STUDY—DAY

*MARTIN is sitting at his desk, typing.*

> NARRATOR (*voice-over*)
>
> He worked steadily for three or four hours, and then he went back to the bedroom to check on Claire.

*Cut to:*


## 39. INT. MASTER BEDROOM—DAY

*A close shot of the fire. The wood is burning less vigorously than before.*

> NARRATOR (*voice-over*)
>
> It was cold that day—much colder than the day before. Diane had been right to worry about the boiler. Martin was supposed to have called Fortunato, but so many things had been happening, it had slipped his mind.

*Cut to:*

*MARTIN is standing over the bed, looking down at CLAIRE. She is asleep.*

*He walks over to the fireplace, crouches down, and puts a log on the fire. It is the last one. He adjusts the logs with an iron poker, working as quietly as he can, but one of the pieces of burning wood inadvertently slips out from under the others.*

*The noise breaks in on CLAIRE's sleep. She stirs, groaning softly as she thrashes about under the covers, and then she opens her eyes. MARTIN swivels around from his spot in front of the fire.*

MARTIN

I didn't mean to wake you. I'm sorry.

*CLAIRE smiles. She looks weak, drained of physical resources, barely conscious.*

CLAIRE

(*Hardly above a whisper*) Hello, Martin. How's my beautiful man?

*MARTIN walks over to the bed, sits down, and puts his hand on CLAIRE's forehead.*

MARTIN

You're burning up.

CLAIRE

I'm all right. I feel fine.

MARTIN

This is the third day, Claire. I think we should call a doctor.

CLAIRE

No need for that. Just give me some more of those aspirins. In half an hour I'll be as good as new.

*MARTIN shakes out two aspirins from the bottle on the bedside table and hands them to her with a glass of water. CLAIRE swallows the pills.*

MARTIN

This isn't good. I really think a doctor should take a look at you.

*CLAIRE finishes drinking the water and hands the glass to MARTIN. He puts it back on the bedside table.*

CLAIRE

(*Taking hold of MARTIN's hand*) Tell me what's happening in the story. That will make me feel better.

MARTIN

(*Touching her face*) You should rest.

CLAIRE

Please, Martin. Just a little bit.

*Not wanting to disappoint her, and yet not wanting to tax her strength, MARTIN confines his summary to just a few sentences.*

MARTIN

It's dark now. Nordstrum has left the house. Anna is on her way, but he doesn't know that. If she doesn't get there soon, he's going to walk into the trap.

CLAIRE

Will she make it?

MARTIN

It doesn't matter. The important thing is that she's going to him.

CLAIRE

She's fallen in love with him, hasn't she?


MARTIN

In her own way, yes. She's putting her life in danger for him. That's a form of love, isn't it?

*CLAIRE doesn't answer. MARTIN's question has overwhelmed her, and she is too moved to give a response. Her eyes fill up with tears; her mouth trembles; a look of rapturous intensity shines forth from her face. It is as if she has reached some new understanding of herself, as if her whole body were suddenly giving off light.*


CLAIRE

How much more to go?


MARTIN

Two or three pages. I'm almost at the end.


CLAIRE

Write them now.


MARTIN

They can wait. I'll do them tomorrow.


CLAIRE

(*Urgently; summoning all her strength*) No, Martin, do them now. You must do them now.

*The camera lingers on her face for two or three seconds—and then, as if propelled by the force of her command . . .*

*Cut to:*

## 40. INT. THE STUDY—DAY

. . . *MARTIN is at his desk, typing. Cut to:*

## 41. INT. MASTER BEDROOM—DAY

*CLAIRE is writhing around on the bed, in acute pain, struggling not to call out for help. Cut to:*

## 42. INT. THE STUDY—DAY

*MARTIN is at his desk, typing.*

*He comes to the bottom of a page, pulls it out of the machine, and rolls in another. He begins typing again. Cut to:*

## 43. INT. MASTER BEDROOM—DAY

*A close-up of the fireplace. The fire has nearly gone out. Cut to:*

## 44. INT. THE STUDY—DAY

*A close-up of MARTIN's fingers, typing. Cut to:*

## 45. INT. MASTER BEDROOM—DAY

*A close-up of CLAIRE's face. She is weaker than before, no longer struggling. Cut to:*

## 46. INT. THE STUDY—DAY

*A close-up of MARTIN's face. At his desk, typing. Cut to:*

## 47. INT. MASTER BEDROOM—DAY

*A close-up of the fireplace. Just a few glowing embers. Cut to:*

## 48. INT. THE STUDY—DAY

*A medium shot of MARTIN at his desk.*

*He types the last word of the story. A brief pause. MARTIN sighs, runs his hands through his hair. Then he pulls the page out of the machine. Cut to:*

## 49. INT. MASTER BEDROOM—DAY

*A medium shot of CLAIRE in bed. She shudders slightly—and then appears to die. Cut to:*

## 50. INT. THE STUDY—DAY

*MARTIN is standing beside the desk, gathering up the pages of his manuscript.*

*He walks out of the study, holding the finished story in his hand. Cut to:*

## 51. INT. MASTER BEDROOM—DAY

*A shot of the doorway.* MARTIN *enters the room, smiling. He glances at the bed, and an instant later the smile is gone.*

*A medium shot of* CLAIRE *in bed.* MARTIN *enters the frame. He sits down beside her, puts his hand on her forehead, and gets no response. He presses his ear against her chest—still no response. In a mounting panic, he tosses aside the manuscript and begins rubbing her body with both hands, desperately trying to warm her up. She is limp; her skin is cold; she has stopped breathing.*

*A shot of the fireplace. We see the dying embers.*

MARTIN *jumps off the bed. Snatching the manuscript as he goes, he wheels around and rushes toward the fireplace. He looks possessed, out of his mind with fear. There is only one thing left to be done—and it must be done now. Without hesitation,* MARTIN *crumples up the first page of his story and throws it into the fire.*

*A close-up of the fire. The ball of paper lands in the ashes and bursts into flame. We hear* MARTIN *crumpling up another page. A moment later, the second ball lands in the ashes and ignites.*

*Cut to a close-up of* CLAIRE*'s face. Her eyelids begin to flutter.*

*A medium shot of* MARTIN*, crouched in front of the fire. He grabs hold of the next sheet, crumples it up, and throws it in as well. Another sudden burst of flame.*

*A close-up of* CLAIRE*'s face. She opens her eyes.*

*A medium shot of* MARTIN*, as before. Working as fast as he can now,* MARTIN *goes on bunching up pages and throwing them into the fire. One by one, they all begin to burn, each one lighting the next as the flames intensify.*

*A medium shot of* CLAIRE. *She sits up. Blinking in confusion; yawning; stretching out her arms; showing no traces of illness. She has been brought back from the dead.*

*Gradually coming to her senses,* CLAIRE *turns her head in the direction of the fireplace. Her expression suddenly changes. She looks stricken.*

CLAIRE

(*Alarm in her voice*) What are you doing? My God, Martin, what are you doing?

*A medium shot of* MARTIN, *as before, continuing to crumple up the pages of the manuscript and toss them into the fire. He turns to her.*

MARTIN

I'm buying you back. Thirty-seven pages for your life, Claire. It's the best bargain I've ever made.

CLAIRE

(*Deeply upset*) But you can't do that. It's not allowed.

MARTIN

Maybe not. But I'm doing it, aren't I? I've changed the rules.

CLAIRE

(*Overwrought; about to break down in tears*) Oh, Martin . . . Martin. You don't know what you've done.

*Undaunted by* CLAIRE*'s objections,* MARTIN *goes on feeding his story to the flames. When he comes to the last page, he turns to her with a triumphant look in his eyes.*

MARTIN

You see, Claire? It's only words. Thirty-seven pages—and nothing but words.

*MARTIN walks over to the bed and sits down. CLAIRE throws her arms around him. It is a fierce and passionate gesture, and for the first time since the beginning of the film, CLAIRE looks afraid. She wants him, and she doesn't want him. She is ecstatic; she is horrified. She has always been the strong one, the one with all the courage and confidence, but now that MARTIN has solved the riddle of his enchantment, she seems lost.*

CLAIRE

What are we going to do? Tell me, Martin. What on earth are we going to do?

*Before MARTIN can answer her . . .*

*Cut to:*


## 52. EXT. THE GROUNDS OF THE HOUSE—DAY

*A series of immobile shots: a tree; a large rock; the trunk of a tree; another tree. Everything is still. No wind is blowing; no air is rushing through the branches; not a single leaf moves.*

*Five seconds go by, ten seconds go by, and then, very abruptly, the screen goes black.*

*Three seconds of total silence, followed by the roar of a speeding car. Fade in:*


## 53. EXT. A COUNTRY ROAD—DAY

*A long shot of a black car driving along a two-lane country road flanked by woods on both sides. Pure wilderness: not a single house or store can be seen. Cut to:*

## 54. INT./EXT. THE CAR—DAY

*MARTIN is driving the car. CLAIRE is sitting next to him in the passenger seat.*

> MARTIN

You'll see. Everything is going to be just fine.

> CLAIRE

(*Apprehensive*) How can you be so sure?

> MARTIN

Because I'm the one who's telling the story. And I can make it turn out any way I like. (*Beat*) This one definitely has a happy ending.

> CLAIRE

(*Smiles; but still worried*) Believe it or not, I've never been to New York.

> MARTIN

Well, we should be there at about eleven o'clock tonight. Assuming the plane leaves on time. (*Beat*) And assuming we don't have a flat tire.

> CLAIRE

Oh?

> MARTIN

I had a flat on the way up, so we're driving with the spare now. Another puncture, and we'll be out of luck.

> CLAIRE

(*Biting her lower lip; thoughtful*) Tell me about New York, Martin.

> MARTIN

What do you want to know?

CLAIRE

Where you live, for one thing. What your apartment is like. Whether it's really big enough for the two of us.


MARTIN

We might have to rearrange some of the furniture, but there's enough room for two people to breathe in there. (*Beat*) If you don't like it, we'll find another place.


CLAIRE

I'm scared, Martin.


MARTIN

Of course you're scared. I'm scared, too. That's the beauty of it. We're going to a place where no one's ever been before. (*Beat*) And I don't mean New York.


*CLAIRE closes her eyes and presses the fingers of her left hand against her forehead. A look of intense concentration. She begins to breathe more deeply, more rapidly, as if she were having some kind of respiratory attack.*


MARTIN

(*Turning to her; growing alarmed*) Are you all right?


CLAIRE

(*Eyes still shut*) Yes, yes. I'm fine.


*Two or three seconds pass; then CLAIRE opens her eyes and begins breathing normally again.*


MARTIN

I still have a lot to learn about you, don't I?

CLAIRE

I have a lot to learn about myself. (*Beat; turning to him with an anguished look*) I hope I don't disappoint you, Martin.

*MARTIN is about to reply—when all of a sudden the rear left tire is pierced by a stone or a nail. As the car begins wobbling and shimmying, MARTIN grips the steering wheel in an effort to bring it under control. Then, putting his foot on the brake, he decelerates, edges the car onto the soft shoulder by the side of the road, and finally comes to a stop.*

MARTIN

(*Pounding the steering wheel in disgust*) I can't believe it. I talk about having a flat tire, and a minute later it happens.

CLAIRE

I'm sorry, Martin. Maybe I'm bad luck, after all.

MARTIN

Sorry? Why should you be sorry? It wasn't your fault.

*Or was it? As MARTIN climbs out of the car to inspect the damage, we wonder if CLAIRE isn't endowed with the ability to exert telekinetic control over inanimate objects. The disruption is similar to the parade of mishaps that occurred during the dinner scene earlier in the film (the broken chair, the spilled salad dressing), and when we remember how conveniently those events spared her from having to answer MARTIN's questions, it seems possible that she might have caused the flat tire as well. But we will never know for sure.*

*CLAIRE gets out of the car and joins MARTIN in front of the rear left tire. We hear air hissing out of the puncture as the tire deflates.*

MARTIN

(*Resigned*) Oh, well. Those are the breaks.


CLAIRE

(*Trying to keep his spirits up*) Not the brakes, Martin. (*Pointing*) That's a tire.


MARTIN *laughs.* CLAIRE *laughs with him.*


CLAIRE (*cont'd*)

(*Turning serious again*) What are you going to do?


MARTIN

There's a gas station a mile or two down the road. I can walk there in about half an hour, buy a new tire, and then have someone from the garage give me a lift back.


CLAIRE

What about me? Don't you want me to go with you?


MARTIN

Of course I do. But there's no point in wearing yourself out. I'll be back before you know it.


CLAIRE

All right, Martin. You do what you think is best.


MARTIN

(*Taking her in his arms and kissing her*) You can take a nap in the car while I'm gone. It will make the time go faster. (*They disengage*) Forty-five minutes. An hour at the most.


MARTIN *turns to leave. He takes several steps . . .*

*A close-up of* CLAIRE.

CLAIRE

Kiss me again, Martin.

*MARTIN goes back to* CLAIRE, *takes her in his arms, and kisses her again.*

CLAIRE *(cont'd)*

You love me, don't you?

MARTIN

*(Kissing her yet again)* What do you think?

*Cut to:*

## 55. EXT. THE COUNTRY ROAD—DAY

*Ten minutes later.* MARTIN *is walking down the road. An eerie silence pervades the landscape: no cars pass, no signs of human life.*

*A wide shot of* MARTIN, *followed by a series of close-ups: his face; a high-angle shot of his feet from his point of view; his eyes. Cut to:*

## 56. INT./EXT. THE CAR—DAY

CLAIRE *is sitting in the passenger seat of the car, smoking a cigarette—looking pensive, ill at ease, taking short, nervous drags and blowing the smoke out the window.*

*A cell phone begins to ring.* CLAIRE *opens the purse on her lap, pulls out the phone, and answers.*

Hello?

*Cut to:*

## 57. EXT. THE COUNTRY ROAD—DAY

*Five minutes later. MARTIN continues walking down the road. After four or five seconds, he stops, crouches down, and ties the laces of his left shoe. He stands up again and resumes walking. The camera observes him from behind as his figure recedes. From a distance, we see him look up.*

*A shot of the sky. Cut to:*

## 58. INT./EXT. THE CAR—DAY

*CLAIRE, still sitting in the passenger seat, holding the cell phone in her right hand. As she listens to her invisible interlocutor, tears are streaming down her face.*

CLAIRE
Yes, I understand. (*Listens*) Good-bye.

*She closes the phone and puts it back in her purse. The tears continue to fall, and she makes no effort to wipe them away. Cut to:*

## 59. EXT. THE COUNTRY ROAD—DAY

*Five minutes later. The camera, positioned twenty yards in front of MARTIN, catches him trotting down the road. He approaches the lens, then sweeps past it. Cut to:*

## 60. INT./EXT. THE CAR—DAY

*Still sitting in the passenger seat, still sobbing, CLAIRE now has a pencil in her hand and is scribbling something on a piece of paper. She looks extremely agitated, on the brink of collapse. Cut to:*

## 61. EXT. THE COUNTRY ROAD—DAY

*Five minutes later. A long shot of MARTIN from behind, still walking down the interminable road. A feeling of the immensity of the space around him: the vault of the cloudless sky, the woods stretching out on either side of the road, mountains towering in the far distance.*

*MARTIN walks, and the camera holds on him until he is nearly engulfed, turned into a speck on the horizon. Just when we are on the point of losing him altogether—*

*Cut to:*

## 62. INT./EXT. THE CAR—DAY

*CLAIRE finishes writing her letter, tears the page out of the notebook, and puts it on the seat beside her. She opens the door and climbs out of the car.*

*With her bag slung over her shoulder, she runs off into the woods. Dissolve to:*

## 63. EXT. THE COUNTRY ROAD—DAY

*A long shot of a rise in the road. Emptiness for two or three beats. MARTIN suddenly appears on the crest, rolling a new tire in the direction of the car.*

*A closer shot of* MARTIN, *struggling to maintain control of the tire as he descends the incline.*

NARRATOR (*voice-over*)

There was only one person at the garage that day—which meant there was no one to drive Martin back to the car.

*A traveling shot of* MARTIN *from the side. The tire has slipped out of his grasp and is bouncing away from him. He runs to catch up with it. After much effort, he finally manages to get his hand on it again, but in so doing he accidentally alters the tire's trajectory. Instead of rolling straight down the edge of the road, it is now angling off in the direction of the woods.*

*Again, the tire eludes* MARTIN's *grasp. It slips onto the soft shoulder, takes a high bounce off a granite rock, and careens into the woods.*

MARTIN *goes charging after it, running in dogged pursuit. After several seconds, the tire crashes into the trunk of a tree and bounds back in* MARTIN's *direction. Unable to get out of the way, he is knocked down. The tire tips over and comes to a stop.*

MARTIN *sits there for several seconds without moving: a slow burn of disbelief and dismay.*

MARTIN

(*Muttering under his breath*) Nice work, Martin.

*Cut to:*

## 64. EXT. THE CAR/THE COUNTRY ROAD—DAY

*A shot of the road. With the car in the foreground, we see* MARTIN *approaching, gingerly rolling the tire with the palm of one hand. Cut to:*

MARTIN *is sitting on the new tire, leaning against the back of the car, holding* CLAIRE's *letter in his hand, reading it for what is no doubt the tenth time. Both the jack and the tire iron are visible, but he has not yet found the courage to begin working. He stops reading and lets his hand fall to his lap. He looks abject, in a state of complete despair.*

NARRATOR (*voice-over*)
He didn't know what to do. If he went home to New York, he felt it would close the book on them forever. Maybe Claire had panicked and would eventually change her mind. If she showed up again, it would have to be in Jack and Diane's house. It was the only place she knew. (*Beat*) And it was Martin's only hope.

*As the narration ends, we hear the sound of an approaching vehicle.* MARTIN *looks up, and a red van enters the frame. The side panels read:* FORTUNATO PLUMBING AND HEAT.

*The van is driven by* JIM FORTUNATO, *a man in his late thirties to mid-forties. He pulls to a stop, sticks his head out the window, and addresses* MARTIN.

FORTUNATO
Need any help?

MARTIN
Thanks. I think I can handle it.

FORTUNATO
Suit yourself. Just trying to lighten your load, brother.

MARTIN *finally notices the writing on the side of the van. He stands up and approaches* FORTUNATO.

#### MARTIN

Fortunato Plumbing and Heat. You wouldn't be Jim Fortunato, would you?

#### FORTUNATO

The man himself.

#### MARTIN

I've been meaning to call you. The boiler in my house is on the blink. It needs to be checked out.

#### FORTUNATO

What house would that be? Can't say I've seen you around here before.

#### MARTIN

I'm just visiting. The house belongs to Jack Restau. You must know him. He's the one who told me to call you.

#### FORTUNATO

Sure, I know Jack. (*Beat*) Why didn't he call me himself?

#### MARTIN

He and Diane are out of the country. They're in Calcutta.

#### FORTUNATO

Calcutta? Wow. (*Beat*) I once read somewhere that the rain in India can come down so hard, the drops are like bullets. If you aren't careful, you can get killed if you go outside. (*Pause; studying MARTIN more carefully*) So what are you, some kind of house-sitter or something?

#### MARTIN

Just a friend. I'm staying in the house while they're gone.

FORTUNATO

Just a friend. And where do you hail from, friend?

MARTIN

New York.

FORTUNATO

New York City?

MARTIN

New York City.

FORTUNATO

That kind of makes you a foreigner, doesn't it?

MARTIN

How so?

FORTUNATO

I once read somewhere that New York is just an island off the coast of Europe. It's not really a part of America.

MARTIN

You do a lot of reading, don't you?

FORTUNATO

All the time. Of all the things in the world, reading is what I like best.

MARTIN

I hope you like fixing boilers.

FORTUNATO

I don't mind it, but it's not what I'd call a passion. You know what I mean?

MARTIN

Do you think you could come out to the house this afternoon?

FORTUNATO

Sorry. I'm all booked up today. Tomorrow's good, though. Sometime after three.

MARTIN

Okay. Tomorrow. Sometime after three.

FORTUNATO

Cheerio, pal. See you then.

*FORTUNATO puts his foot on the gas pedal and speeds off, raising a cloud of dust and gravel in his wake. Fade out.*

*Fade in:*

## 65. INT. THE COUNTRY HOUSE—DAY

*From the entrance hall of the house, a shot of the front door.*

NARRATOR (*voice-over*)

So he went back to the house . . .

*The door opens, and in walks MARTIN carrying his suitcase. As he closes the door behind him:*

NARRATOR (*voice-over*)

. . . and the second part of the story began.

*MARTIN walks into the living room.*

MARTIN

(*Looking around*) Claire?

*The camera follows him into the living room.*

MARTIN

Claire?

*MARTIN enters the kitchen.*

MARTIN

Where are you, Claire?

*Cut to:*


## 66. INT. THE HALLWAY—DAY

*One by one, as we listen to the sound of* MARTIN*'s footsteps in the hall, we see his right hand pulling open the door of each room and then slamming it shut. A frantic, rapid-fire series of jump cuts.*

*First: the spare bedroom. Second: the master bedroom. Third: the study. Fourth: the bathroom. Dissolve to:*


## 67. INT. MASTER BEDROOM—NIGHT

MARTIN*, still dressed, is lying in bed with his eyes closed, fast asleep. We can barely make him out in the dimness.*

*The camera pushes in on his face for a close-up. Fade out.*

*Fade in:*

## 68. INT. IMAGINARY BEDROOM—THE DREAM

*MARTIN is lying in bed, as before—but the room is no longer dark. The colors on screen have been desaturated, giving the images an unreal, otherworldly look.*

*A knocking is heard at the door. MARTIN opens his eyes, rolls out of bed, and walks to the door. From this point on, the door is the only object visible in the scene: a door suspended in black space. The camera moves between CLAIRE and MARTIN, at times showing them both simultaneously, at other times just one, cut off from the other.*

### CLAIRE

Martin. Martin, are you awake?

### MARTIN

(*Excited, exuberant*) Claire!

*He reaches for the doorknob and turns it, fully expecting the door to open at once. But it doesn't. The door is mysteriously locked, and no matter how hard MARTIN turns and pulls at the knob, he is unable to open it. He rattles the door on its hinges, but still nothing happens. In frustration, he pounds on the surface with his fist.*

### MARTIN (*cont'd*)

I can't open it! I'm locked in!

*CLAIRE is standing on the other side of the door, her ear pressed against the surface. She is wearing a pink version of her black cocktail dress and high heels.*

### CLAIRE

Don't worry about the door, Martin. I just want to make sure you're all right.

MARTIN

All right? No, I'm not all right. (*Pause; in a plaintive, agonized tone of voice*) What happened, Claire? Why did you run away?

CLAIRE

You shouldn't have left me alone, Martin.

MARTIN

What was I supposed to do? We couldn't go to the airport without the car, could we? And the car needed a new tire.

CLAIRE

They called me back. I didn't have any choice. As long as you were there, they'd lost their hold over me. But then you walked away, and suddenly I was powerless again.

MARTIN

But we broke the spell. I brought you back to life. Once that happened, I thought you'd be free of them forever.

CLAIRE

That's what I thought, too. But I was wrong.

MARTIN

So what happens now?

CLAIRE

I'm being punished.

MARTIN

For how long?

CLAIRE

I don't know. Everything is in chaos. They've never been faced with a situation like this, and no one knows what to do. They've been arguing about it ever since you burned your story.

MARTIN

(*Bitterly*) Good. Let them suffer, too. Just because I'm a puny, good-for-nothing schmuck with a typewriter, that doesn't mean I can't fight them.

CLAIRE

Why do you want me so much, Martin? There are other women in the world, you know.

MARTIN

I've been with other women, Claire. I was even married once. (*Beat*) You're the first person . . . I've ever cared about more than I care about myself. It's that simple.

*CLAIRE, moved by MARTIN's declaration, gently strokes the door with her fingers, then brings her face up against the wood and kisses it. Fade out.*

## 69. INT. MASTER BEDROOM—DAY

*The next morning. MARTIN wakes up with a start. He looks around him— confused, disoriented, afraid. Cut to:*

## 70. INT. THE STUDY—DAY

*MARTIN is sitting at the desk. The surface is bare: no typewriter, no paper, no pencils and pens—all of them presumably stored away prior to his departure with CLAIRE.*

*He opens one of the drawers and removes the yellow legal pad, which he places before him. Then, shutting the first drawer, he opens another and removes a ballpoint pen, which he places on top of the pad. He closes the second drawer, picks up the pen, and begins to write.*

*All the while, we have been listening to the voice of the* NARRATOR.

NARRATOR (voice-over)

The next morning, Martin decided to write down everything he could remember about the time he'd spent with Claire. If he concentrated hard enough on the past, maybe it would teach him what to do in the present.

*Cut to:*

## 71. MONTAGE

*We see a number of scenes that took place earlier in the film—from* MARTIN'S *point of view. This time, however, they are shown in black and white and run in slow motion without sound:*

1. MARTIN and CLAIRE's first encounter in the bedroom, each holding up a key to the house and showing it to the other.
2. Talking and drinking wine in the living room that evening.
3. CLAIRE stripping off the Berkeley T-shirt.
4. MARTIN running his hand along CLAIRE's naked back.

*Cut to:*

## 72. INT. THE KITCHEN—DAY

*MARTIN is sitting at the kitchen table with a half-finished bowl of soup in front of him—which he ignores. Instead, he is holding the letter that CLAIRE left for him in the car.*

*MARTIN puts down the letter, pushes away the bowl of soup, and then leans forward and rests his head on his arms.*

*A medium shot of MARTIN from behind.*

*CLAIRE quietly enters the frame, looks down at MARTIN for a few moments, and then begins stroking his hair. Eventually, she bends over and kisses the crown of his head.*

*A closer shot of MARTIN from behind. He jerks up his head, wheels around, and looks into the camera.*

*A longer shot of the same. CLAIRE is nowhere to be seen.*

*After a moment, a knocking is heard at the front door. Cut to:*

## 73. INT. THE FRONT HALLWAY—DAY

*MARTIN opens the front door and is confronted by a grinning FORTUNATO. Toolbox in hand, the plumber is dressed in green work clothes. The monogram on his shirt reads JIM.*

FORTUNATO

Am I too early? (*Beat*) Am I too late?

MARTIN

No, no. The timing's perfect.

*FORTUNATO enters the house briskly and walks in the direction of the hall.*

FORTUNATO

No need to show me the way. I've been here dozens of times.

MARTIN

Do you want some help?

FORTUNATO

(*Stopping in his tracks*) Don't worry. I know that boiler better than my own mother. (*Beat*) That's because I was an orphan.

*FORTUNATO laughs at his own joke, then continues on his way toward the hall. Cut to:*


## 74. INT. THE LIVING ROOM—DAY

*Half an hour later. With his back to the camera, FORTUNATO is examining the books in the bookcase.*

*A close-up of his hand reaching for a volume:* The Burning House, *by Martin Frost.*

*In a wider shot, we see FORTUNATO flipping through the pages of the book. He comes to the author photo on the inside back flap of the dust jacket. A close-up of MARTIN's face.*

*At that moment, MARTIN enters the room, holding a check in his hand. He approaches FORTUNATO.*

Here's your money.

*He gives the check to FORTUNATO, who takes it with his right hand. With his left hand, he holds up the book and shows it to MARTIN.*

FORTUNATO

You're a writer. A published novelist.

MARTIN

So it would seem.

FORTUNATO

(*Thrusting out the check, which has MARTIN's name printed on it*) Martin Frost . . . (*thrusting out the book*) . . . and Martin Frost. I thought there was something familiar about your face. I just couldn't remember where I'd seen it.

MARTIN

You're not going to tell me you've read my work.

FORTUNATO

I could lie to you and say I have, but I've heard of you.

MARTIN

Well, at least that's something.

FORTUNATO

More than something. Forgive me if I gape, but I'm a little in awe.

MARTIN

Get a grip on yourself, Mr. Fortunato. It will pass.

FORTUNATO

No, I mean it. You see, I'm a writer myself. Not a published one, but a scribbler just the same.


MARTIN

(*By now vaguely amused*) Oh? What kinds of things do you write?


FORTUNATO

Stories, mostly. Short stories. All kinds of stories. Science fiction. Horror. Whodunits. Political thrillers. Erotica.


MARTIN

How can you be so prolific and run a business at the same time?


FORTUNATO

Energy, Mr. Frost. Days, I grapple with pipes, toilets, and boilers. But at night I withdraw into my imagination. You'd be amazed how much a man can accomplish when he sleeps only two or three hours a night. It gives him enough time to live two lives, to be two men in a single body.


MARTIN

What's the secret? If I slept that little, I'd pass out on my feet.


FORTUNATO

Passion. Ambition. Desire. (*Pause; studying Martin; nervously*) I don't mean to impose, Mr. Frost . . .


MARTIN

Call me Martin.


FORTUNATO

Not Marty?

Martin.

FORTUNATO

All right, Martin, then call me Jim. No more of that Mr. Fortunato
stuff.

MARTIN

Okay. Jim. (*Beat*) You were saying?

FORTUNATO

Yes. (*Beat; mustering his courage*) I don't mean to impose myself on you,
Martin, but I was wondering if you had the time to take a look—just a
little peek, really—at some of my . . . some of my output.

MARTIN

I don't know if my opinions are worth that much, but sure, why not?
I might be in for a pleasant surprise.

*Cut to:*


## 75. INT. MASTER BEDROOM—NIGHT

*MARTIN is asleep in bed, under the covers. Fade out.*


## 76. INT. IMAGINARY BEDROOM—THE DREAM

*Desaturated colors, as previously.*

*This time MARTIN is already standing, his ear pressed against the door.*

MARTIN

How long has it been going on?

CLAIRE

Years, Martin. Many, many years. But you were my first writer.

*CLAIRE's ear is pressed against the door as well. Once again, she is wearing the pink version of her cocktail dress.*

CLAIRE *(cont'd)*

I always used to be sent to painters and musicians. But then there was a bad incident, and I was reassigned.

MARTIN

What happened?

CLAIRE

Last year in Paris, a painter named Philippe Malebranche hanged himself in his studio.

MARTIN

I remember reading about that. He did it because of you?

CLAIRE

It wasn't my fault. I was his model, not his lover. When the painting was finished, I had to leave. I always leave after the work is finished. He couldn't handle it, and a month later he killed himself.

MARTIN

I know just how he felt.

CLAIRE

Don't get any foolish ideas, Martin. I'm fighting for us every day. The story isn't over yet.

MARTIN

What if I broke down the door? What if I grabbed hold of your hand and pulled you into the room?

CLAIRE

It wouldn't do any good. The moment you stepped into the hall, I wouldn't be there anymore. The dream would be over.

MARTIN

I don't know how much longer I can take this, Claire.

CLAIRE

They're still squabbling over what to do with me. There's so much confusion, they're starting to make mistakes. Matching up women with the wrong men. Men with the wrong women.

MARTIN

(*Ironic*) And men with the wrong men. Not to speak of women with the wrong women.

CLAIRE

(*Smiles*) As a matter of fact, yes.

MARTIN

And?

CLAIRE

I don't know. But if we manage to help them fix the mess, maybe we can make a bargain with them.

MARTIN

"We"? How can I do anything?

I don't know, Martin. Time will tell.

*Fade out.*


## 77. EXT. THE GROUNDS OF THE HOUSE—DAY

*The next morning. A close shot of a leaf, followed by a close shot of wildflowers. An exact reprise of Scene 6. Cut to:*


## 78. INT. THE STUDY—DAY

*MARTIN is sitting at the desk, writing furiously. He comes to the bottom of a page in the yellow legal pad, then flips it over and begins writing on the next one. Cut to:*


## 79. MONTAGE

*As the narration begins, another sequence of black-and-white images from the past, running silently in slow motion:*

1. CLAIRE putting on the Hume T-shirt, then peeling it off and embracing MARTIN.
2. CLAIRE revolving on the rope swing.
3. CLAIRE sprinting across the grass, pursued by MARTIN.
4. CLAIRE swimming in the pool.
5. CLAIRE's wild laughter at the end of the dinner scene.

Martin sensed that things were changing. The more he wrote about Claire, the more he felt her presence in the house. He was not someone who believed in ghosts. He had always been a rational person, but there were times when he could have sworn he felt her breathing beside him. Were the words he was writing about her actually bringing her back? Martin was afraid to think such a thought. He couldn't allow himself to hope anymore. But without hope, why was he still in the house? Why was he still writing the story?

*Cut to:*

## 80. INT. THE LIVING ROOM—DAY

*MARTIN is sitting in a chair with his eyes closed, apparently asleep. His right arm is flung out to the side, and on the floor, just below his hand, we see a few scattered pages from the sports section of* The New York Times.

*The camera pulls back, and CLAIRE enters the frame. She approaches MARTIN, falls to her knees in front of him, and lays her head on his chest. Very gently, she begins stroking his face.*

*A close-up of MARTIN. He opens his eyes.*

*A longer shot of the same. CLAIRE is nowhere to be seen.*

*After a moment, a knocking is heard at the front door. Cut to:*

## 81. INT. THE FRONT HALLWAY—DAY

*MARTIN opens the door. FORTUNATO is standing on the threshold, wearing a tweed sports jacket, a pale blue shirt, and a blue-and-yellow-striped tie. His hair is neatly combed. This sartorial change has turned him into someone who resembles a college professor. To complete the effect, he is holding a leather brief- case in his left hand.*

FORTUNATO

(*Eagerly*) Is this a good time? (*Beat*) Is this a bad time?

*Cut to:*


## 82. INT. THE LIVING ROOM—DAY

*MARTIN is sitting on the sofa. FORTUNATO has settled onto the adjacent sofa. He reaches into the briefcase and pulls out three typed manuscripts of various lengths, then tosses the briefcase aside and puts the stories on his lap.*

FORTUNATO

I didn't want to overwhelm you, so I decided to bring just three. What you might call a representative sampling of my work. (*He glances down at the pile on his lap, picks up the first manuscript, and waves it at Martin*)

This one is called "The Little People of Lastmania." Lastmania is a fictitious republic in central Europe, hidden away in the Carpathian Mountains. Population three and a half million. Principal crop: the potato. One year, the harvest fails and famine spreads through the coun- try. Dr. Anatole Karpak, Lastmania's leading scientist, goes to the pres- ident with a plan to save the country. The problem is: too little food, too many people, right? Not enough *resources*. Karpak has analyzed the situation, and his conclusion is that the Lastmanians are too big. I'm talking about their bodies. Their bodies are too big. They need too much food to sustain them, and since there isn't enough food to go around, he's invented a pill that can shrink people to one-third their original size. Swallow the pill, and a six-foot man becomes a two-foot man. If a six-foot man can survive on nine potatoes a day, a two-foot man needs only three. Get it? There are enough *resources*.

MARTIN

Incredible.

FORTUNATO

Actually, it's an allegory about the environmental crisis in the world today. We're destroying the planet because of greed, because everybody wants too damn much. Too many cars, too many power plants, too many washing machines. The only way we can save the earth is if we start thinking *small*.

MARTIN

What are the other stories about?

FORTUNATO

(*Holding up the second manuscript*) This one's called "Kiss My Ass, Sucker." The hero's a private dick named Don Sharp, a classic hard-boiled gumshoe. Lots of fast talk, lots of fisticuffs.

MARTIN

And the third one?

FORTUNATO

(*Holds up the third manuscript*) This one's my latest. I just finished it last night, and it's probably the best thing I've ever done. "Bushwhacked." That's the title. (*Opens the manuscript to the first page*) How do you like this for a first sentence? (*Reads*) "It was the morning of George W. Bush's third inauguration." (*Closes the manuscript; grins at MARTIN*)

MARTIN

Promising.

91

FORTUNATO

"Bushwhacked." (*Gesturing with his hand as he separates the two elements of the compound word*) Bush . . . whacked. Get it? The story's about a conspiracy to assassinate the son of a bitch who calls himself our president.

MARTIN

You don't like old George, huh?

FORTUNATO

I despise the bastard. He's a dangerous liar, and he's done more to hurt America than any man in our history.

MARTIN

I didn't know there were any Democrats up in this neck of the woods.

FORTUNATO

Democrat? Who's a Democrat? I hate those cruds, too.

MARTIN

Oh?

FORTUNATO

I vote Socialist Labor. I'm a one-hundred-percent, dyed-in-the-wool Trotskyite.

MARTIN

One of the last of a dying breed.

FORTUNATO

Permanent revolution, Martin. It's the only answer to the world's problems.

MARTIN

What about "thinking small"?

FORTUNATO

I was talking about natural resources. When it comes to politics, you have to think big.

*MARTIN glances at his watch.*

FORTUNATO *(cont'd)*

I'm boring you.

MARTIN

No, not in the least. I'm just a little tired, that's all.

FORTUNATO

If you want my opinion, you look kind of down. There's this sad look in your eyes, Martin.

MARTIN

I finished a new novel a few weeks ago. It always takes me a couple of months to recover.

FORTUNATO

So you're not writing anything now?

MARTIN

A little. *(Beat)* I'm taking notes. *(Beat)* Getting ready for the next thing.

FORTUNATO

And other than that, you just hang around this big old house. All alone, with no one to talk to. *(Beat)* No wonder you're depressed. What you need is a little diversion.

MARTIN

Maybe.

FORTUNATO

(*His face brightening*) Have you ever heard of Screwdriver Darts?

MARTIN

Screwdriver Darts?

FORTUNATO

It's a game Jack and I invented. It's great fun, Martin. Maybe I'll come around sometime and teach you. You know . . . (*Gesturing to the stories*) . . . as a way of thanking you for reading my stuff.

*Dissolve to:*

## 83. INT. THE STUDY—DAY

*The next morning. Tipped back in his chair, his feet on the desk, MARTIN has the yellow legal pad on his lap and is reading over what he has written so far. First one page, then another, then another . . .*

*Cut to:*

## 84. MONTAGE

*Another sequence of black-and-white images from the past, running silently in slow motion:*

1. CLAIRE fainting on the grass, as seen through the window of MARTIN's study.

2. CLAIRE in her sickbed.
3. A close shot of MARTIN's hands throwing crumpled pages into the fire and burning his manuscript.
4. CLAIRE opening her eyes and coming back to life.

*Fade out.*


# 85. EXT. THE SKY—NIGHT

*A shot of the moon in the sky.*


# 86. INT. MASTER BEDROOM—NIGHT

*A close-up of MARTIN lying in bed, asleep.*

*A wide shot of the room. CLAIRE tiptoes in, barefoot, dressed in a skimpy nightgown.*

*A closer shot of the bed. CLAIRE slips under the covers and embraces MARTIN from behind. With his eyes still shut, MARTIN rolls over and puts his arms around her. They begin to kiss, to fondle each other.*

*After ten seconds, a close-up of MARTIN's face. He opens his eyes.*

*A shot of MARTIN's hand reaching for the switch of the lamp on the night table.*

*The room fills with light.*

*MARTIN sits up and looks around. No one is there.*

*He buries his face in his hands. Cut to:*

## 87. INT. THE FRONT HALLWAY—DAY

*A tight shot of the front door opening.* FORTUNATO *is standing on the threshold, dressed in an elegant gunslinger's outfit—straight from a vintage Hollywood western. Black cowboy hat; black cowboy boots; black shirt; black leather vest; black pants; black belt with a silver buckle; white bolo tie with a silver clasp; a gun belt with two thin holsters, each one holding two long screwdrivers with white handles.*

FORTUNATO

(*Smiling*) Hi, Martin. Ready for some fun?

MARTIN (*off*)

That's some getup.

FORTUNATO *steps into the house. The camera backs up as* MARTIN *closes the door.*

FORTUNATO

(*Spreading out his arms*) The official uniform for Screwdriver Darts.

MARTIN

You mean Jack has one of those, too?

FORTUNATO

You bet. But his is white.

MARTIN

I hope you don't mind if I forgo the pleasure . . . and stick to my own clothes.

FORTUNATO

(*Patting* MARTIN *on the shoulder*) No problem. Whatever you like.

*They exit the frame,* FORTUNATO *in front,* MARTIN *trailing behind. Cut to:*

## 88. EXT. THE GROUNDS OF THE HOUSE—DAY

*Several minutes later.* MARTIN *and* FORTUNATO *approach the back wall of an outbuilding on the property. A round wooden target (resembling an archery target) is fastened to the wall.*

*A close-up of* FORTUNATO's *hand reaching for four screwdrivers on top of the wall. They are identical in size to the ones in* FORTUNATO's *holsters. The only difference is that their handles are black, not white.*

*A wider shot of the two men.*

> **FORTUNATO**
> (*Handing the black-handled screwdrivers to* MARTIN) These are Jack's. I'm sure he won't mind if you use them.

> **MARTIN**
> (*Grinning at the absurdity of it all*) Let me guess. (*Points*) The object is to hit that target.

> **FORTUNATO**
> Exactly. Forty points for red—the bull's-eye. Twenty points for the blue ring. Ten points for the white ring. Five points for the yellow ring. First one to get to a hundred wins. We play for fifty dollars a game.

> **MARTIN**
> Fifty dollars? (*Beat*) You and Jack take this thing seriously, don't you?

> **FORTUNATO**
> If there's no risk, there's no enjoyment.

MARTIN

Where do you stand?


FORTUNATO

(*Points; begins walking away from the back wall*) Right here. Behind this line.


*He points to the ground, where indeed a number of evenly placed stones have been set out on the grass. They are approximately eighteen feet from the target. MARTIN walks over and joins FORTUNATO at the line.*


MARTIN

(*Looking at the target*) It's pretty far, don't you think?


FORTUNATO

This isn't regular darts, Martin. It's Screwdriver Darts. And to get a screwdriver to stick in that wooden target, you have to throw it with incredible force.


*Without another word, FORTUNATO positions himself behind the line and removes a screwdriver from his right holster. Gripping the screwdriver by the blade, he raises his hand above his head and zings off a mighty throw—the equivalent of a ninety-mile-an-hour fastball. The screwdriver lands in the white ring with a resounding thud.*


MARTIN

Pretty impressive.


FORTUNATO

(*Disappointed to have missed the bull's-eye*) Just warming up. (*Beat*) Why don't you give it a try?


*MARTIN positions himself behind the line.*

MARTIN

How do you hold it? By the handle or the blade?

FORTUNATO

The blade. You get better balance that way. A single half turn between the line and the target.

*MARTIN raises his right arm, steadies himself in concentration, and lets off a throw. By some miracle, the screwdriver lands in the red bull's-eye.*

FORTUNATO

(*Patting MARTIN on the back*) A star is born. (*Beat*) You're a natural, Martin.

MARTIN

(*Smiling*) Very satisfying . . .

FORTUNATO

Do you think you're ready for a game?

MARTIN

Why not?

*Dissolve to:*

*A close-up of the target. One after the other, a succession of white-handled and black-handled screwdrivers come flying into the frame. More than half of them bounce off the wood and fall to the ground. Others stick in the various rings. Three or four hit the bull's-eye. This sequence should last approximately twenty seconds. Cut to:*

*MARTIN and FORTUNATO are walking toward the target to collect their screwdrivers after their most recent tosses.*

FORTUNATO

(*Shaking his head*) I'm really sorry, Martin. After that first throw, I thought you were going to be a lot better at it.


MARTIN

Beginner's luck. And then reality set in.


*They collect their screwdrivers.* MARTIN*'s are lying on the ground. All of* FORTUNATO*'s have landed in the target.*


FORTUNATO

(*Yanking out a screwdriver, then another*) I hate to take your money.


MARTIN

Forget it. You won, I lost. Fair is fair.


FORTUNATO

(*Yanking out two more screwdrivers*) But five hundred dollars. It's too much. (*Beat*) Especially after all you've done for me.


MARTIN

I haven't done anything for you.


FORTUNATO

I know you haven't read my stories yet. But you will. You're a man of your word, and you're not going to let me down.


MARTIN

Come on into the house, and I'll write you a check.


MARTIN *puts the black-handled screwdrivers on top of the wall and begins walking toward the house.* FORTUNATO *follows close on his heels.*

FORTUNATO

(*Enthusiastically*) I've got it. I'll let you have my niece, Anna.


MARTIN

Your niece? What are you talking about?


FORTUNATO

I just don't feel right taking all that money and not giving you something back.


MARTIN

I still don't understand what this has to do with your niece.


FORTUNATO

She's eighteen years old and has no job. She can cook for you, clean the house, do the laundry. I'd like to offer you that in exchange for the money.


MARTIN

That's very kind of you, Jim. But I'd rather not.


FORTUNATO

(*Disappointed*) With Anna around, you won't be alone in that big old house anymore.


MARTIN

But I like being alone. (*Beat; emphatically*) I want to be alone.


*Cut to:*

## 89. INT. THE LIVING ROOM—DAY

*MARTIN is sitting in a chair, reading one of FORTUNATO's stories.*

*Eventually, he lets out a small grunt and tosses the manuscript on the floor. The camera pans to the title page: "The Little People of Lastmania" by James Fortunato.*

## 90. EXT. THE GROUNDS OF THE HOUSE—DAY

*A shot of the rope swing, followed by a shot of the empty swimming pool. After a moment, the NARRATOR begins to speak.*

> NARRATOR (*voice-over*)
> There was nothing more to write . . . nothing more to think. All he could do now was wait . . . or else give up, pack his bags, and leave.

*Cut to:*

## 91. INT. THE STUDY—DAY

*A shot of the yellow legal pad lying on MARTIN's desk. Accompanied by the sound of wind blowing through the trees.*

## 92. EXT. THE GROUNDS OF THE HOUSE—DAY

*MARTIN is alone, practicing Screwdriver Darts. Sweat pours down his face. He has clearly been at it for some time.*

*He throws the first screwdriver toward the target. It bounces off the wall and drops to the ground.*

*He throws the second screwdriver toward the target. Same result. Ditto the third and fourth.*

*A close-up of the screwdrivers lying on the ground. Fade out.*

## 93. INT. THE KITCHEN—DAY

*MARTIN is standing at the kitchen sink, washing dishes.*

*A knock is heard at the front door. MARTIN turns off the water, hastily dries his hands with a towel, and leaves the room. Cut to:*

## 94. INT. THE FRONT HALLWAY—DAY

*MARTIN opens the door—and once again FORTUNATO is standing in front of him. This time he is dressed in a black tuxedo, with a starched white formal shirt, a black bow tie, and pearl-studded cuff links. Behind him, we can see a young woman, ANNA JAMES, walking away from the house. She is wearing rumpled, loose-fitting clothes; her long hair is tousled, unkempt; and her movements are unsteady: the clumsy, wobbling walk of a blind person or a drunk.*

MARTIN

You again.

FORTUNATO

(*Grinning*) I'm going to a banquet at the governor's mansion, and I wanted you to see my duds before I left. (*Gesturing with his hands*) Pretty spiffy, huh?

103

MARTIN

The governor's mansion?

FORTUNATO

A few months ago, I saved a little girl from drowning. Maggie Fitzsimmons. Maybe you heard about it on the news. Now I'm getting the official state medal for heroism and bravery.

MARTIN

(*Referring to* ANNA) Who's that?

FORTUNATO

(*Wheeling around; addressing* ANNA *sharply*) Not that way, stupid. Come into the house. (*Turning back to* MARTIN) That's my niece. Anna.

ANNA *turns around and begins to approach the door—still wobbly, still listing back and forth on her feet. Her disheveled hair hangs down over her eyes and nose, obscuring her face.*

MARTIN

I thought I told you—

FORTUNATO

(*Interrupting* MARTIN; *apologetically*) I know, I know. But when I mentioned coming over here yesterday, she said she wanted to meet you. She wouldn't take no for an answer.

*The camera backs up as* FORTUNATO *and* ANNA *enter the house.*

FORTUNATO (*cont'd*)

(*Addressing* ANNA) Say hello to Martin.

ANNA

(*Looking down at the floor; in a barely audible voice*) Hello, Martin.

MARTIN

(*Trying to be polite*) Hello, Anna.

*MARTIN extends his hand to her, but she doesn't take it.*

FORTUNATO

(*Addressing ANNA*) Shake his hand, dummy.

*As if too exhausted to lift her arm, ANNA gives MARTIN a weak, limp-wristed shake.*

FORTUNATO (*cont'd*)

(*Addressing ANNA; pointing to the living room*) Now go sit down on the sofa.

*ANNA mutely obeys FORTUNATO's command. The camera follows her as she stumbles forward into the living room and plops herself down on the sofa. Like someone in a trance, she sits there without moving, looking down at the floor.*

*By now, MARTIN and FORTUNATO have entered the living room as well. They are standing side by side, at some distance from ANNA, who remains visible in the background.*

MARTIN

What's wrong with her? She looks half-dead.

FORTUNATO

It's a sad story, Martin. (*Beat*) She turned up on my doorstep about nine months ago with nothing but the clothes on her back. Homeless, penniless. I had to take her in, didn't I?

MARTIN

What happened? Did she run away from her parents?

FORTUNATO

That's the problem. She has no parents. My sister and her husband, Al James, were killed in a car crash in Oregon last year.

MARTIN

(*Growing disturbed*) Are you telling me her last name is the same as your first name?

FORTUNATO

Yeah. So what? It's just a coincidence.

MARTIN

(*Pursuing the thought*) When was the last time you saw Anna before she showed up at your house?

FORTUNATO

Way back. She couldn't have been more than two or three. (*Beat*) My sister and I weren't very close.

MARTIN

How do you know that Anna is your niece?

FORTUNATO

Of course she's my niece. Why else would she have come to me?

MARTIN

I don't think she's a real person, Jim.

FORTUNATO

(*Flummoxed*) What are you talking about?

MARTIN

She's a spirit . . . a phantom being.

*FORTUNATO is so mystified by MARTIN's statement, he cracks up laughing.*

#### FORTUNATO
You're nuts, Martin. (*Beat*) That's the craziest thing I ever heard.

#### MARTIN
(*Trying to stay calm*) When did you start writing your stories?

#### FORTUNATO
(*Thinks*) I don't know. About a year ago, I guess.

#### MARTIN
But you didn't get serious about them until Anna started living with you. Isn't that right?

#### FORTUNATO
(*Exasperated*) I thought you were a smart person, Martin. I looked up to you. I wanted to be your friend. But what you're saying now is just plain stupid.

*FORTUNATO walks over to ANNA.*

#### FORTUNATO (*cont'd*)
(*Addressing MARTIN; pointing at ANNA*) Look at her. You call that a spirit? She's a flesh-and-blood human being—and a royal pain in the ass to boot. When she started living with me, she weighed a hundred and sixty pounds. Now look at her. She's as skinny as a stick. She barely eats anything, she barely talks to me, and she's never shown me the slightest bit of gratitude for taking her in. Not one word of thanks. (*Addressing ANNA*) Stand up, birdbrain.

*ANNA stands up.*

FORTUNATO (*cont'd*)

Now slap me across the face.

*Without hesitation, ANNA hauls off and slaps him across the face. She lets out a small, contented giggle.*

FORTUNATO (*cont'd*)

(*Rubbing his cheek*) You see what I mean? She likes to hurt me. She enjoys it.

MARTIN

If you don't want to get slapped, you shouldn't ask her to do it.

FORTUNATO

I'm just showing you what she's like, that's all. The girl's an idiot. She barely knows how to read and write, and you can see . . . (*Gesturing*) . . . how beautifully she takes care of herself. (*Beat*) But, believe it or not, she has the voice of an angel. (*Addressing ANNA*) Take the hair out of your face.

*ANNA does as she is told. She turns out to be remarkably lovely.*

FORTUNATO (*cont'd*)

Now sing one of your songs.

*The moment ANNA opens her mouth, we understand that FORTUNATO was telling the truth. She has an exquisite voice.*

ANNA

(*Sings*)

       I'm the girl you can't see
       I'm the girl who isn't me

I sail the seven seas of my heart
And where love ends is where I start
To China, to London, to Rio, to France
I'll live the life and dance the dance
And even if you climbed aboard, my friend
I wouldn't give you another chance
'Cause I'm the girl you couldn't see
'Cause I'm the girl who wasn't me.


MARTIN

(*Deeply impressed*) How did you learn to sing like that?


ANNA

(*Smiling for the first time*) I don't know. I just woke up one morning, and I could do it.


FORTUNATO

(*As if showing off a highly trained pet dog*) She can sing . . . and she can also act. (*Addressing* ANNA) Anna. Do one of your monologues for Martin.

*Once again,* ANNA *delivers an outstanding performance. Her previous languor and clumsiness have disappeared. She is animated, vibrant, in full control of herself.*


ANNA

(*As Portia, from Act III, scene ii, of* The Merchant of Venice)

You see me, Lord Bassanio, where I stand,
Such as I am: though for myself alone
I would not be ambitious in my wish,
To wish myself better; yet, for you
I would be trebled twenty times myself;

A thousand times more fair, ten thousand times more rich;
That only to stand high in your account,
I might in virtues, beauties, livings, friends,
Exceed account . . .


### MARTIN

(*Again, deeply impressed*) Portia, from *The Merchant of Venice*. Right?

ANNA *nods.*


### MARTIN

Excellent.

ANNA *gives* MARTIN *a small smile. Then she sits down in the chair and immediately lapses into her earlier state of lethargy and disorientation.*

FORTUNATO *glances at his watch.*


### FORTUNATO

Christ. I have to get moving. The reception starts at six, and I have a long drive ahead of me. (*Addressing* ANNA) Come on, Anna, let's go. I'll take you home.


### ANNA

I want to stay with Martin. I'll cook and clean for him, just the way you said I could.


### FORTUNATO

(*Peeved*) But Martin doesn't want a cook. I already told you that.


### ANNA

I don't care. I like it here. And I like Martin.

*FORTUNATO walks over to ANNA and grabs her arm.*

FORTUNATO

Come on, dumbbell. Enough's enough.

*Appalled by FORTUNATO's rough treatment of her, MARTIN comes to a sudden decision.*

*A close-up of MARTIN's face.*

MARTIN

I've changed my mind, Jim. She can stay if she wants to. (*Beat*) At least for now. We'll give it a couple of days and see how it works out.

*Cut to:*


## 95. INT. THE KITCHEN—DAY

*Twenty minutes later. MARTIN and ANNA are sitting at the kitchen table, drinking coffee. We catch them in midconversation.*

MARTIN

Where did you come from, Anna?

ANNA

From Jim's house.

MARTIN

Before that. I mean, where were you before you went to Fortunato's?

ANNA

(*Drinks the last of her coffee; puts the cup down on the table*) I can't remember. (*Beat*) It rained a lot.

MARTIN

Oregon?


ANNA

Maybe. (*Thinks*) They never told me.


MARTIN

"They"? Who do you mean by "they"?


ANNA

The people I lived with. (*Closes her eyes and presses her fingers against her temples, trying to concentrate. As if talking to herself*) It's funny. I can't see them anymore.


MARTIN

How old are you, Anna?


ANNA

(*Opens her eyes; thinks*) I'm not sure. (*Beat*) Sometimes I think I was just born. Like about ten minutes ago. Do you know what I mean?


MARTIN

(*Lets out a sigh, as if to signal he is abandoning the interrogation*) Do you promise to eat when I give you food?


ANNA

Yes. I promise.


MARTIN

All right. What I want you to do now is go down the hall and take a bath. Then go into the master bedroom. You'll find women's clothes in the closet. Put on anything you like. Okay? Do you think you can handle it?

ANNA

(*Pause*) I think so.

MARTIN

If anything goes wrong, just give a shout.

*ANNA smiles.*

ANNA

Like this? (*Shouting*) Help! Help!

MARTIN

Exactly. Just like that.

*Cut to:*


## 96. INT. THE HALLWAY—DAY

*From behind, we see ANNA walking down the hall. To the left, several feet ahead of her, the bedroom door opens—and out steps CLAIRE. She smiles at ANNA.*

CLAIRE

Hello, Anna. Would you like me to help you?

ANNA

Who are you?

CLAIRE

My name is Claire. (*Beat*) I'm here because of Martin.

ANNA

I don't understand.

CLAIRE

Don't worry. I'll explain everything.

CLAIRE *takes* ANNA *by the hand and leads her toward the bedroom.*
*Cut to:*

## 97. INT. THE LIVING ROOM—DAY.

MARTIN *is sitting on the sofa, reading a magazine.*

ANNA *enters the room. She has been utterly transformed. Her hair washed,*
*combed, and pulled back from her face, she is wearing a pair of tight-fitting*
*black jeans and a blue silk tunic. In her right hand (for reasons that will soon*
*be made clear) she is holding a red scarf.*

MARTIN

(*Glancing up; studying her in amazement*) Look at you. (*Long pause*) Now
that's what I call an improvement.

ANNA *smiles, then does a slow 360-degree turn.*

ANNA

Thank you. I couldn't have done it myself.

MARTIN

(*Perplexed*) What does that mean?

ANNA *sits down on the adjacent sofa.*

ANNA

Claire helped me. (*Beat*) She's a very nice person, you know.

MARTIN

(*Astonished*) Where is she?


ANNA

Do you want to see her?


MARTIN

Of course I want to see her.


ANNA

I'm sorry. I shouldn't have said that. What I meant was: do you want to talk to her?


MARTIN

Is there a difference?


ANNA

You're not allowed to look at her. If you do, she'll disappear and never come back.


MARTIN

(*Thoughtful*) I've really screwed things up, haven't I?


ANNA

What you have to do is blindfold yourself with this scarf. Then you can talk to her as long as you want.


MARTIN

Can I touch her?


ANNA

I think so. But I'm not sure.

*MARTIN puts on the blindfold.*

CLAIRE (*off*)

Of course you can touch me, Martin. You can even kiss me if you want to.

*MARTIN stands up and reaches out his arms, groping blindly.*

MARTIN

Where are you?

*CLAIRE walks straight into his arms.*

CLAIRE

Right here, Martin.

*MARTIN and CLAIRE embrace; then they begin to kiss . . .*

*Dissolve to:*


## 98. EXT. THE GROUNDS OF THE HOUSE

*Some time later. As the camera slowly pans the tops of the trees in the garden, we hear:*

CLAIRE (*off*)

It was the best I could do. No one has ever wanted to stay before. There's no precedent, and they didn't know how to handle it.

MARTIN (*off*)

I still don't understand why I can't look at you.

CLAIRE (*off*)

Because I belong to you, Martin. To you and no one else. (*Pause*) For the time being, I'm trapped between here and there. They said it would go on like this for a year.

MARTIN (*off*)

And what happens after the year is up?

CLAIRE (*off*)

If all goes well, you'll be able to look at me again. That was the implication, in any case.

*Cut to:*

*MARTIN and CLAIRE are sitting on a bench in the garden. She is on his lap with her arms around him. He is still wearing the blindfold.*

CLAIRE (*cont'd*)

They're not always as clear as they could be.

MARTIN

And how do you define "going well"?

CLAIRE

For one thing, you have to take care of Anna. That's how I managed to talk them into it. She was sent here by mistake. She wasn't ready, and now she needs an education. She needs to be taught how to become a person.

MARTIN

But Anna lives with Fortunato. He thinks she's his niece.

CLAIRE

I don't think Mr. Fortunato will have any objections.

No?

No. (*Beat*) He's a terrible writer, isn't he?

I'm afraid so.

The poor girl. That's why we have to do everything for her we can. We have to undo the damage, and then she can go back and start again.

(*Pondering the future*) Hmm. This is getting complicated. (*Beat*) What else?

*CLAIRE kisses MARTIN on the lips.*

No sex. No sex for a year.

Not even with the blindfold?

No, Martin. Only in your dreams.

(*Thinking; remembering*) But those aren't dreams. They're real.

*A close-up of CLAIRE's face. She breaks into a big smile. Fade out.*

# 99. EXT. OUTSIDE THE HOUSE—DAY

*The next morning.* CLAIRE *and* ANNA *are loading suitcases into the trunk of the car. Because* MARTIN *is wearing the blindfold, he is unable to help.*

CLAIRE *slams the door of the trunk shut.*

> CLAIRE
> (*Giving* ANNA *a hug*) I think you're all set.

ANNA *climbs into the front passenger seat of the car.* CLAIRE *walks over to* MARTIN *and puts her arms around him. He hugs her back.*

> MARTIN
> I wish you were going with us now. It doesn't make any sense for you to stay behind.

> CLAIRE
> I can't go now. But I'll join you in New York later.

> MARTIN
> When?

> CLAIRE
> Soon. I promise.

> MARTIN
> (*Still hugging her*) I don't want to let go of you again.

> CLAIRE
> You have to. (*Beat*) I wish I could go now, too, but I can't.

*They kiss, then* CLAIRE *leads the blindfolded* MARTIN *to the door on the driver's side. She opens the door for him, and* MARTIN *slides in behind the wheel.*

CLAIRE

(*To* ANNA) Bye, Anna.

ANNA

Bye.

MARTIN

One more kiss.

*CLAIRE leans over and kisses him on the lips. Then she shuts the door.*

CLAIRE

Drive safely, Martin.

*Instead of walking away, CLAIRE unexpectedly opens the back door and sits down behind MARTIN.*

## 100. INT./EXT. THE CAR—DAY

MARTIN

(*Sitting behind the wheel; still blindfolded*) Claire? Is that you sitting in the back?

CLAIRE

Yes, Martin.

*She shuts the door.*

MARTIN

How can I drive to New York with this scarf around my eyes?

CLAIRE

Take it off.

MARTIN

If I do that, I'll see you in the rearview mirror. And then I'll lose you.

CLAIRE

No you won't. (*Beat*) I wanted it to be a surprise. (*Beat*) Mirrors don't count.

MARTIN

(*Doubtful; afraid*) Are you sure?

CLAIRE

Positive.

*CLAIRE slowly removes the blindfold.*

*She and MARTIN look at each other in the mirror. They begin to smile.*

MARTIN

Hello, Claire.

*A close-up of CLAIRE.*

CLAIRE

Hello, Martin.

*Fade out.*


## 101. INT. ANYWHERE

*The screen is filled with a single image: MARTIN's typewriter, hovering in black limbo.*

*Although the keys don't move, we hear the steady, insistent sounds of typing. Dissolve to:*

## 102. INT. MARTIN'S STUDY—DAY

*A close shot of* MARTIN'*s fingers, typing quickly. Dissolve to:*

*We see* MARTIN'*s face. He is looking out at the garden from the window in his study. A small, mysterious smile begins to form on his lips. His eyes register a wistful contemplation. After a few moments, we hear:*

> CLAIRE *(off )*
>
> Why don't you sing us a song, Anna?

> ANNA *(off )*
>
> What do you want to hear? Something slow and sad—or fast and funny?

> CLAIRE *(off )*
>
> Anything you like.

> MARTIN *(off )*
>
> Fast and funny.

## 103. EXT. A COUNTRY ROAD—DAY

*We see the black car from a distance, speeding along an empty country road. Waves of fog pour down from the mountain behind.*

ANNA *begins to sing "Polly Wolly Doodle."*

*The car exits the frame.*

ANNA *continues to sing. When she comes to the end of the first verse, the screen goes black.*

*A brief pause, and then the final credits begin to roll.*